PENGUIN BOOKS
THAT'S INCURABLE!

George Thomas and Lee Schreiner are pseudonyms for two physicians at Harvard Medical School who ought to know better. One of them was taught by the other, though neither can remember who taught what to whom. Both are actively involved in medical research, usually as prisoners. Their numerous awards and honors include Second Place in the 1982 Nobel Prize Bake-Off (Nobel, Indiana). They now occupy staff positions of considerable importance—or so they are led to believe. Their current chief ambition is not to get fired.

OTHER TITLES BY THE SAME AUTHORS

Suture Self
Grayish Anatomy
A Farewell to Arms and Legs
The Whines of Wards
From Here to Maternity
On Death and Diet

That's Incurable!

The Doctors' Guide to
Common Complaints,
Rare Diseases,
and the Meaning of Life

*by George Thomas, M.D.,
and Lee Schreiner, M.D.*

**ILLUSTRATIONS BY
JACK ZIEGLER**

PENGUIN BOOKS

Penguin Books Ltd, Harmondsworth,
Middlesex, England
Penguin Books, 40 West 23rd Street,
New York, New York 10010, U.S.A.
Penguin Books Australia Ltd, Ringwood,
Victoria, Australia
Penguin Books Canada Limited, 2801 John Street,
Markham, Ontario, Canada L3R 1B4
Penguin Books (N.Z.) Ltd, 182–190 Wairau Road,
Auckland 10, New Zealand

First published 1984

Copyright © George Thomas and Lee Schreiner, 1984
Illustrations copyright © Jack Ziegler, 1984
All rights reserved

LIBRARY OF CONGRESS CATALOGING IN PUBLICATION DATA
Thomas, George.
  That's incurable!
    1. Medicine—Anecdotes, facetiae, satire, etc.
I. Schreiner, Lee.   II. Title.
R705.T48   1984   610'.207   83-17378
ISBN 0 14 00.7021 4

Printed in the United States of America by
R. R. Donnelley & Sons Company, Harrisonburg, Virginia
Set in I T C Cheltenham

Grateful acknowledgment is made to International Creative Management, Inc., for
permission to quote a selection from *Ondine* by Jean Giraudoux, English version
by Maurice Valency. Copyright, as an unpublished work, 1951, 1953, by Maurice
Valency. Copyright 1954 by Maurice Valency. Acting edition copyright ©
Maurice Valency, 1956.

Contents

Introduction

The right to dissemble; to speak freely of your symptoms without restraint; to bare arms or for that matter anything else to the doctor of your choice at the hour of your choice—thus would the Constitution have enshrined your rights as a patient if our forefathers hadn't been off nursing their lumbago with leeches. After all, good health has always been part of the American dream. In a society where happiness could truly be pursued and eventually cornered, medical care would be readily available to all who wanted it, without costing them their savings or dignity.

As we all know, however, American medicine falls far short of this lofty ideal. Emergency rooms do not have welcome mats or promote a Happy Hour. Hospitals don't offer getaway weekends (although one can occasionally arrange a cruise-to-nowhere). Federal laws do not forbid physicians from rolling their eyes. Instead we have a health care system that cruelly provides intensive care to the patient only when he needs it. When he finally starts getting the attention he's been seeking, he's too sick to enjoy it.

One reason is that there just aren't enough doctors to go around. There are fewer than 400,000 physicians in the United States, and at any given time about a quarter of them are tied up working on their backhands. Another twenty percent are busy applying for grants. Many of the rest are psychiatrists, who may just be making matters worse.

Competing for the attention of these doctors are over 200 million Americans. Of these, about 517 feel fine and live in Maine. They need not be counted in calculations of how health care is distributed. Many others, who are genuinely ill, are poor, can't speak English, or don't know anybody, and thus have difficulty gaining access to care. They don't count either. Still, there have always been lots of folks left over trying to elbow their way into the waiting room. The situation has been a near-crisis since the 1960s, when Medicare moved old people off the ice floes and back into society.

The forgotten victims of this crush have been those sometimes cruelly labeled as hypochondriacs. These gentle souls harm no one and never ask for much—just reassurance, understanding, a Medic-alert bracelet, and their doctor's home phone number. In less turbulent times, they were respected members of the community, who were prized for their ability to identify poisonous plants. Gradually, though, these patients have come to feel that they are not welcome when they show up in their doctor's office. Little things add up. No more free pills, for example. And while some patients are encouraged to undress almost immediately, these patients are not even allowed to unbutton their overcoats. Some find it significant that before they are shown into the doctor's office, he has had all the chairs removed. They have been forced into a kind of underground, where they subsist on tofu, vitamin C, and Adelle Davis books.

Recently, though, doctors have noted a new militancy among these patients. All over the country, they are taking charge of their own decaying bodies. They're tired of scorn; they will no longer tolerate condescension. So what if doctors call them hypochondriacs? They argue convincingly that hypochondriasis is not a disease, though almost everything else is. "Pills, not ill will" is their motto. They've stepped out of the medicine cabinet and into the emergency ward.

Sociologists are hardly surprised, for in so many ways, this movement is the logical sequela to Vietnam, Watergate, and the Me Decade. It is the final preoccupation with the self—flavored by the assumption that the self is sick, or at least headed in that general direction. As in Vietnam, American technology can raise a lot of hell, but irresistible forces are irresistible forces. In the end, these patients know, is the end. They don't need to ask, "Death, where is thy sting?" They know where it is. Right there. In the back seat.

This book was inspired by fervent requests from such patients for more and more information. They would bring us a common complaint and want to know the worst possible disease it could represent. We gave them simple, unambiguous answers in terms that they could understand.

Their tears of gratitude moved us. Eventually, though, performing this service of compassion became a tedious bore, even after we added dance steps and made them beat time with a reflex hammer. Thus we began to circulate mimeographed sheets simply listing the most popular complaints, along with our estimate of how much time the sufferer might have left if things went badly (e.g., "runny nose—3 months").

Soon our patients were not satisfied with the mundane. They wanted the low-down on the rarest of syndromes with the most innocuous of initial symptoms—diseases they were better off not knowing about. They wanted to know about infections they could catch from their pets; about how exercise can take years off your life and render the time left behind miserable. They wanted to know how to recognize their own psychiatric emergencies; how they could examine themselves when no one else would; and how to get into the hospital when they felt lonely. They didn't want to know about the possibility of dying from an allergic reaction during sex, but we told them anyway.

Thus this little volume became what it is today—a handbook for hypochondriacs. It is the fruit of our looms, a general guide by which to live, full of the medical background you need to manipulate your doctor and loved ones. Every disease described is real. No punches are pulled. No data are falsified. Each of the studies mentioned, and medical information presented, is absolutely true, though lots of it is twisted and taken out of context.

This book will teach you about dozens of diseases that you almost surely do not have. Still, they have been carefully chosen so that your doctor will have a hell of a time ruling them out once you have raised the possibility. He will be forced to put you through an extensive evaluation, perhaps requiring a hospital admission. If the workup is entirely negative, the chances that you have some other fatal disease are slightly reduced, assuming that the tests themselves don't bump you off.

These tests will be expensive, of course, which raises the question of how you should regard the cost crunch in U.S. health care. The sad fact is that we live in a time of diminishing resources and increasing needs. You should make every attempt to ignore this bad news. Endless worrying about how society is going to pay for your stomach X rays is only going to upset your stomach. You must consider the health care system a precious resource, like our national parks, and visit it as often as possible.

It has been written that the road to bad health is paved with good intentions. With the purchase of this book, you have made the first, faltering move. Now, if you'll just follow us, we'll show you the rest of the way.

That's Incurable!

Common Complaints and the Worst Possible Diseases They Could Represent

Ever since man first discovered his own mortality, he has been seeing it behind every rock, tree, and bush. Naturally, this insight has changed the way he looks at the world and his all-too-precarious place in it. Man did not become less contemplative—he merely started contemplating different things: sores that were slow to heal, for example, or subtle changes in bowel and bladder habits. The meaning of life suddenly seemed less pressing an issue than the question of how to prolong it. The intense desire to understand one's role in a universe supervised by unseen and powerful gods became secondary to the intense desire to understand what in the hell was causing that red, itchy rash between the toes.

Before doctors were created, man sought to master these bodily complaints through religion. Indeed, some believe that the word "symptom" is derived from a Greek phrase meaning "My throat is sore; call the priest." Patients tried various rituals to fend off the aches and pains of ancient life. Smearing mud in one's hair, solemn chanting, and eating an apple a day all seemed promising at first, but eventually proved false hopes. Once they found that no church had a prayer for irregularity, they gave up on religion altogether.

At first medicine could do no better. In ancient cultures, doctors did not understand the physiology behind diseases any more than priests did. They were full of purpose, but short on power—and had little to offer or even do.[1] As far as we can tell, physicians in early Greece had no function in their day other than concocting suicide potions and practicing their putting in a special area of the temple.

Chinese physicians were the first to try to pick up the early warning signs of doom—though not by choice. An early emperor decided that paying doctors when you were sick made little sense. It seemed more logical to pay the physician only when you were well. When the emperor himself felt poorly, he made his court physicians feel even worse. He put them to death.

The court physicians, a group naturally prone to nervousness, took to dropping in on the emperor every day just to see how things were going. Legend has it that a few of the younger doctors, fresh out of Chinese medical school, began coming by every thirty minutes, until the emperor had two of them put away for breathing too heavily on his feet.

Since that shaky start, doctors have learned a great deal about symptoms and their implications. Patients, too, have discovered the importance of keeping up with the latest insights into the body's imperative to reproduce and deteriorate, though not necessarily in that order. Thus, today, everyone knows that if your tongue is too smooth, you could have pernicious anemia, resulting in low blood counts and dementia; that bad breath can mean gangrene of the stomach; or that insomnia may mean cirrhosis of the liver, caused by confusing Miller Time with Daylight Savings Time.

Instead of such routine fare, this chapter will focus on some com-

---

[1] Much like first-base coaches.

mon complaints and the worst possible diseases they could respresent. The worried patient need no longer be afraid to present his blemish or discharge to the modern doctor, only to have his concern scorned as groundless fear. This chapter and this book will put some solid ground under your fear. Now, instead of asking the doctor what *he* thinks of that symptom you have been observing and perhaps nursing when it threatened to falter, you can tell the doctor what *you* think of it. The two of you will get on as never before.

Pins and Needles

Almost everyone has had a hand or foot "go to sleep." Usually this sensation is due to pressure on a limb's blood vessels and nerves, and represents your body's way of crying "Uncle!" The pins-and-needles feeling passes after the pressure is relieved by, for example, uncrossing your legs, or making your brand-new lover wake up and get off your arm.

But what if your hand went to sleep and never woke up? Next time, before the sensation passes, remember that this sort of numbness can be an early sign of leprosy.

Most Americans think they have come no closer to leprosy than Ben Hur reruns, and, even then, as far as they were concerned, Charlton Heston couldn't stay far away enough from his mother and sister in the Valley of the Lepers. Few realize that there are still ten to twenty million lepers in the world, with the chief areas of concentration in the United States being New York, Florida, Louisiana, Hawaii, Texas, and California, especially along the border areas. (Leprosy remains one of Mexico's chief exports to this country.)

The first signs of leprosy are usually patches of skin that are darker or lighter than surrounding areas, but many cases begin with numbness. These changes are due to infiltration of the skin with *Mycobacteria leprae,* a distant cousin of the bacteria that cause tuberculosis, though neither will own up to the relationship. Fingers and noses fall off sometime thereafter.

Cases of advanced leprosy are rarely seen today, and this disease is now less a medical danger than a psychological one. Effective drug therapy is widely available, and researchers have found that leprosy can be communicated to another only after prolonged exposure. Etiquette books continue to suggest that if your date complains that her foot has fallen asleep, wave good-bye through tinted glass instead of kissing her goodnight. Such recommendations, however, may be overly cautious.

Nevertheless, the social stigma surrounding this disease persists, and a sudden cry of "Leper!" will still empty a movie theater. Leprosy's victims are understandably touchy on this issue. They have organized themselves into support groups that offer psychological counseling and are now campaigning to change the name of their affliction from leprosy to the less familiar and less inflammatory Hansen's disease.

Don't be fooled.

Frequent Urination

The question comes up all the time, and is raised by people of all ages: the child who needs three "rest stops" on the New Jersey Turnpike; the student taking an exam who makes four trips to the bathroom, generating charges of cheating; the young woman who excuses herself over and over during the course of an evening, leaving her date to wonder—Can this be normal?

Incredibly, the answer is yes.

How often someone needs to make what doctors call "Number One" depends on many factors, including the volume of fluid they drink and how much of it includes caffeine, which increases urine output. Coffee has cut short thousands of conversations, while Pepsi has spoiled *The Sorrow and the Pity* for a generation of film fans. And, of course, we all know the effect of alcohol on urination, which is well summarized by the First Law of Kidney Physiology: "You don't buy beer; you rent it."

But as with so many bodily functions, increased frequency of urination can be an early warning sign of a serious illness, or—more likely—evidence that it is already too late. Thus careful patients keep track of the time, amount, and general quality of each voiding, and insist on discussing this data with their physicians once a week.

While no one really knows how many trips to the bathroom per day are "normal"—a value-laden term, and a concept that has outlived its usefulness—most doctors accept the following:

1. The adult male bladder holds about one pint of urine and the female bladder slightly less. Some patients do have a diminished capacity, but not all of them have cancer.

2. The average urine output per twenty-four hours is about three pints.

3. For comfort, for dignity, and sometimes just for something to do, most adults void when their bladder is half full (or half empty, if you wish)—or five to six times per day.

4. Assuming about one minute per voiding, the average person spends three months of his life urinating and six months washing his hands afterward.

In other words, we "piss away," as it were, a period equivalent to our junior year at college—for many of us, the best year of our lives. Those who void more often are losing even more precious time—yet another reason to monitor this important bodily function carefully.

The most common cause of increased frequency in women is an infection of the urinary tract, a well-known variant of which is "honeymoon cystitis." The infection begins in these women shortly after sexual intercourse—apparently during all the commotion down there, bacteria climb up into the bladder. Decades of research and millions of dollars have been spent in study of this problem, but our understanding of it has progressed little beyond the conclusion of the anatomists who originally described the syndrome: "God put the water-works too close to the playground."

Unfortunately, increased frequency of urination can also herald the onset of more serious diseases. Some of them are common, such as diabetes mellitus, in which a high blood-sugar level robs the kidneys of the ability to concentrate urine. Thus diabetics find themselves constantly urinating, and, because of the sugar that is "spilled" in their output, their urine is sweet to the taste—which is the oldest way of diagnosing diabetes. (This technique has been replaced by modern technology, thank God.)

A rare form of diabetes, diabetes insipidus, has nothing to do with high blood sugar. This illness is caused by tumors of the pituitary gland, which is located in a rather sensitive area of the brain, about two inches behind the eyes. As these tumors grow, they destroy cells that produce a hormone needed by your kidneys to concentrate urine. Without the hormone, you urinate five gallons a day or more of almost pure water. In the Middle East, these patients are admired for their ability to make the desert bloom, but elsewhere, this condition has its drawbacks.

These tumors also press on other structures, especially the optic nerves. Usually, the first deficit that evolves is loss of peripheral vision. So if you are urinating more and enjoying it less, ask yourself:

1. Do I get headaches?
2. Am I having trouble seeing things way off to the side?

If the answer to both these questions is no, then the chances that you have a pituitary tumor are slightly reduced.

The Sniffles

A runny nose, or rhinitis, is usually due to a cold or exposure to an allergen, such as pollen. Consequences are generally limited to making you an unpopular person to sit with for more than thirty seconds.

Sometimes, though, rhinitis is prolonged and can signal a sinus infection or more serious condition. Among these are Lethal Midline Granuloma (described in slightly more detail in the chapter "Ten Diseases You Were Better Off Not Knowing About"); Wegener's Granulomatosis (an inflammatory disease that can erode the nasal septum and damage the lungs and kidneys); congenital syphilis; and leprosy. None of these is going to help you win friends and influence people.

Then there is the possibility that what is running out of your nose and onto your sleeve is not mucus at all, but cerebrospinal fluid—the clear liquid that surrounds and bathes the brain. With skull fractures, cerebrospinal fluid can leak out into the nasal passages. The danger lies not in loss of the fluid, but in spread of bacteria from the nose into the brain. What then ensues is the microorganism's equivalent of the Oktoberfest.

Physicians have a quick test to distinguish cerebrospinal fluid from mucus—they just measure the liquid's protein levels, which will be quite high if the liquid is mucus. So if you are concerned about your runny nose, simply mail a sample of your discharge to your doctor. He will be glad to tell you whether he thinks you should have your head examined.

Night Blindness

Patients constantly wonder whether they are getting enough of their essential vitamins. They are especially concerned about vitamin A, because A comes at the beginning of the alphabet, suggesting that this vitamin must have unusual importance.

And they are right. Vitamin A, which is found in many vegetables, is crucial to normal vision. True deficiencies usually manifest themselves first with a complaint of night blindness and can almost always be traced to dietary inadequacies or gastrointestinal diseases causing an inability to absorb the vitamin. Irreversible damage to vision can occur if these problems are not corrected.

So when patients say they are concerned about their vitamin A levels, we suggest that they ask themselves, "Do I have trouble seeing in the dark?" If the answer is yes, they may be deficient in vitamin A and should consider taking a supplement, or at least eating some vegetables once in a while. Just don't overdo it. Vitamin A overdoses can be dangerous, and these patients should be on the alert for the signs of toxicity—headache, pain in the joints, loss of hair, large sheets of skin peeling away, kidney and liver damage, that kind of thing.

After offering this counseling, we tell patients that they are on their own.

Excess Saliva

Production of too much saliva, also known as ptyalism, is often ascribed by laymen to carelessness or lack of control. In fact, ptyalism can be a manifestation of a number of illnesses that affect salivation nerve centers located in the lower brainstem. Drooling can be induced by encephalitis (inflammation of the brain), rabies, botulism, arsenic poisoning, or rare degenerative nerve diseases. Any one of these possesses the ability to transform a person's mind into something resembling anchovy paste.

If you are not sure if you suffer from ptyalism, spit one day's production of saliva into a container and send it to your doctor so he can decide whether you're drooling a little or a lot. If you use Federal Express, you can be sure it will get there overnight. Repeat once a week as a precaution, until your doctor promises you will never get sick or until he is forced to move to an area not serviced by Federal Express.

Ringing in the Ears

Tinnitus, or ringing in the ears, is usually due to wax in the ear's external canal. That is a disgusting enough situation for anyone to confront, not to mention embarrassing for everyone involved. Most doctors are more at ease telling a patient he has cancer than an earful

of wax. The cancer patient feels less guilty about his diagnosis—appropriately so.

Still, doctors wish that all cases of tinnitus were due to ear wax, for life would be so much simpler then. If a patient came in complaining of ringing in the ears, we'd know that we should not examine them without rubber gloves. Unfortunately, almost any disorder of the ear can cause this problem, including infections and trauma from noise at work or rock concerts.

The most feared cause of tinnitus is a tumor of the nerve to the ear —an acoustic neuroma. Because of the strategic location of this nerve inside the skull, the tumor can raise a lot of hell if allowed to grow. Fully excluding this possibility requires a rather expensive set of X rays involving considerable radiation exposure and personal attention.

Go for it.

Headaches

Rare as brain tumors are, almost everyone has heard a horror story about one, like that of George Gershwin. One day, the great composer of *Rhapsody in Blue* had a headache; the next, some difficulty in finishing a concert. A few months later, he was dead from a glioblastoma.

People like George Gershwin give headaches a bad name.

Actually, most headaches don't have anything to do with the brain, other than being at the same end of the body. They arise from tension of the muscles under the scalp and face, or, as in migraine headaches, spasms of blood vessels in the head. Bad as they are, they eventually pass.

There are, of course, serious and potentially fatal causes of headaches, impossible for the layman to separate from the garden-variety sort induced by screeching children. Among them are brain tumors, meningitis, and end-stage syphilis.

Bad as these disorders are, doctors are troubled even more by the fear that a headache may represent a subdural hematoma. These hematomas, or blood clots, begin with a tear of the veins inside the skull, usually after head trauma. This trauma can be as mild as bumping one's head on the bottom of the dinner table while picking up a dropped fork. The torn veins will usually repair themselves, but sometimes they continue to leak, and the clot slowly expands. Eventually, the brain gets squeezed over to one side, or out the hole in the bottom. Not surprisingly, this pressure causes headaches.

In one case, a nearly fatal subdural was attributed to a fall on the ice almost twenty-five years before the clot was finally detected. Of course, if you haven't bumped your head in the last quarter century, you have little to worry about. As a precaution, we personally never pick up eating implements we drop at dinner. We don't get invited back often, but we sleep better at night for it.

Head Size

Is your head too large?

If so, you may have Paget's disease, a bone disorder found in about three percent of Americans over 40. In this poorly understood disease, normal bone is replaced by abnormal, poorly formed, and bulkier bone—sometimes in one or two areas, occasionally everywhere.

Most patients never know they have Paget's disease, but others notice a swelling or deformity of a limb, and may limp as one leg lengthens. Those with Paget's of the skull find that their hat size increases. Later, headaches can be severe, and the new bone can choke off nerves from the brain to the ear. Occasionally, involved bone at the base of the skull compresses the spinal cord, leading to paralysis.

Promising treatments for Paget's disease are now under development, making it worthwhile for you to check your own skull circumference periodically. Weekly measurements plotted on a graph can be very helpful to your physician.

Hiccups

Hiccups represent a complex reflex that follows irritation of the respiratory muscles—especially the diaphragm—or the nerves connecting them to the brain. Most episodes have no obvious cause and pass after several uncomfortable and embarrassing hours, during which even your closest friends will avoid you.

Occasionally, though, hiccups are a sign that something more ominous is afoot, in which case we call them hiccoughs. Pneumonia and liver tumors can both irritate the diaphragm, while brain tumors and viral encephalitis—an infection of the brain—can induce hiccoughs from above. Heart attacks involving the bottom of the heart, which rests on the diaphragm, can also be accompanied by hiccoughs. Sometimes these humiliating little noises are the first sign of heart disease.

Some people like to try curing hiccups by "scaring" the patient with sudden noises. These tactics actually work in some cases. You should keep in mind, however, that if the patient is indeed having a heart attack, you might just kill him.

Drowsiness

If you have become drowsy while reading this section, do not be alarmed. Sleepiness is experienced by most people much of the time, and by President Reagan almost all the time. It is particularly associated with the alpha and omega of human existence—sexual intercourse and large meals, both of which should immediately be followed by a long nap. The unifying theme in these superficially disparate activities is that of movement: movement of the earth during the former, movement of the colon during the latter. (In an unfortunate few, movement of the earth during climax and of the colon during digestion are functionally linked. These are the ones who are asked to leave Boy Scout Camp within a week of their arrival.)

Drowsiness during other activities, such as watching televised proceedings of the United Nations or listening to the annual Christmas radio broadcast of dogs barking "Jingle Bells," may be a warning that you are about to die in your sleep. This fate is particularly frightening, because it cruelly denies the patient one of life's most fulfilling moments: telling the doctor he was wrong when he said you didn't have a fatal disease.

For example, you could be coming down with an infection by a virus that feeds on your frontal lobes—St. Louis encephalitis. Contrary to popular belief, you can't get it by using a toilet seat there. The virus is carried by mosquitoes, who leave it behind when they bite. Then the microbes travel right to your head and proceed to disassemble your silicon chips. By the time they finish, your brain looks like a neurological version of the South Bronx. The expression "room at the top" takes on a new meaning for you and your friends.

More popular causes of drowsiness are failure of the liver (cirrhosis) and of the kidneys. When those organs precede you across the Great Divide, the poisons they normally clear from your blood are sopped up by your brain like dirty dishwater in a paper towel. Why does this make you sleepy? Because the poisons gum up the works, to use technical terms. It is an ironic commentary on our state of evolution that anything we can't urinate immediately gets stored in the brain. This phenomenon may be the best explanation we have for the condition of the U.S. Senate.

Then there's the Kleine-Levin syndrome. This extremely rare disorder has no known cause and tends to attack younger people. It is manifested by recurrent episodes of sleepiness, excessive hunger, restlessness, irritability, and a destructive degree of mental confusion. It is sometimes mistaken for a much more common, and more painful, malady—male adolescence. There is no cure for victims of either disorder. They should be put to sleep by a veterinarian amid peaceful surroundings.

Blue Navel

The navel is an often unappreciated feature of the otherwise bland expanse of one's abdomen. Like those Swiss weather-prediction toys (when the gnome is pink, it's going to rain; when the gnome is black, sell gold), it can be a beacon that signals the inner chaos of your intestines.

A suddenly blue navel, for instance, is typically regarded by patients as a laughable curiosity, something to show the boss during a dull lunch hour. In reality, a blue navel can signify either of two impending disasters. It can mean that there is a large amount of blood in your abdomen due to rupture of a big, big blood vessel. In this case, forget about impressing the boss; you're not going to collect on those bonus vacation days.

Alternatively, a blue navel can mean you have pancreatitis, an inflammation of the gland behind your stomach that looks like filler but is actually vital to normal digestion. Usually, pancreatitis is due to overindulgence in alcohol. A pancreas exposed to too much alcohol can blow up faster than a cockroach in a microwave oven.[2]

Thus we tell our patients that, after a three-martini lunch with an important client or the company president, take off your shirt or zip down your dress and quickly check the color of your navel. A little forethought on your part will allow you to plan the rest of day or evening around a possible trip to the emergency room. If you are drinking during an evening of romance, a navel check may well start the ball rolling, especially if it is presented in the context of preventive medicine.

Fatigue

Fatigue is a normal physiological response to exertion, mental or physical. But it is also a normal physiological response to poisoning with *Clostridium botulinum*—better known as botulism.

As everyone who gets a little nervous around vichyssoise or Grandma's peach preserves knows, botulism is transmitted in improperly canned foods. The *Clostridia* bacteria secrete a powerful toxin that usually dissolves in prolonged, intense heat. Sometimes, though, a breakdown in the heating process allows the poison to survive. The results are deadly.

Fatigue develops first, usually about one day after exposure. Eventually, neuromuscular disturbances lead to double vision, difficulty in swallowing or talking, and weakness. Typically, the mind remains clear to the end. Two thirds of cases are fatal.

---

[2]Thirteen seconds.

In the United States, the most common sources of botulism are canned vegetables, seafood, pork, and beef. Thus, we tell our patients to delete these in any form—canned or fresh—from their diets. Instead, they should choose their foods from one of these five basic groups:

1. Encapsulated foods. Health-food stores offer a variety of tasty snacks and gourmet dinners in handy tablet or capsule forms.

2. Foods whose origin cannot be determined by their appearance. Foods in this group include tofu, organic egg salad, and pâté. They have no shape or definable color or taste.

3. Food that cannot be easily separated from its wrapper. If you are having so much trouble getting through, it is going to be much harder for bacteria, which have no hands and a poor sense of direction.

4. Foods derived from petroleum by-products rather than grown in dirty dirt. Once available only along the New Jersey Turnpike, such foods are now easily found all over the country. Some examples: vending-machine pastry, ballpark hot dogs, any bread that has a smiling woman on the wrapper, and nondairy creamers—all of which rise in price during oil embargoes.

5. Chili.

If you insist on purchasing a canned product, bring an ice pick to the supermarket. Stick it into your prospective purchase and hold the can up to your ear to listen for escaping gas. Hold a match near the hole. Shake the can and look for foam. Do not buy any can that emits flammable gas when punctured. If the supermarket employees approach you with a few questions, wave the ice pick wildly at them.

Irritability

Any kind of mood swing or personality change, even if it initially seems like an improvement, may actually be caused by a serious brain disorder or an accumulation of toxins. Patients will often think that they are just out of sorts or have turned over a new leaf, when in fact they will soon be pushing up daisies. Such cases give rise to the medical dictum, "A new you may be the last you."

Specifically, irritability may be an early sign of rabies or tetanus— two diseases that would have been invented by parents to terrify children had they not already existed. Thus, grouchy patients should regularly search their homes and workplaces for rusty objects upon which they might cut themselves. They should also daily examine their dogs for evidence of excessive drooling—in which case they should immediately have the animal put to sleep.

Sweating

There is little good to say about sweat. Even in a normal, healthy person, perspiration is dangerous. Besides the devastation it wreaks on social intercourse, there is the constant threat of dehydration and electrolyte disturbances, which can cause fainting spells and even cardiac arrest. Fear of these consequences explains why physicians avoid any activity likely to produce perspiration.

If the picture painted by the information in this chapter has depressed you, that's appropriate, for if history has taught us anything, it's that everything can be bad news. Even feeling good can be bad. Patients occasionally glide into our offices exuding a sense of well-being, of fulfillment, of confidence in their physical and mental health. All too often this euphoria is the beginning of the end.

Many deadly diseases are capable of producing a giddiness that patients confuse with that much rarer entity, true happiness. For example, adrenal or pituitary tumors secrete toxic levels of corticosteroids, causing a "steroid high" that fills the patient with a mysterious energy and ironic joy.

Inappropriate elation can also mean that the brain is running on too little oxygen, suggesting major-league problems with the heart and lungs. High concentrations of oxygen may bring these patients back to earth, but the underlying diseases are usually so serious that resuming a normal life is out of the question. Patients remain on the ground only for a brief refueling before continuing their flight.

Thus if you find yourself feeling extraordinarily well, we recommend getting to a hospital immediately. It may already be too late.

Ten Diseases You Were Better Off Not Knowing About

Few tasks in a doctor's life are as emotionally trying as telling a patient who is convinced he is ill that nothing is wrong. The ensuing hostilities can be brutal, but then no one ever promised that medicine would be pretty. Most physicians eventually learn how to handle the common, everyday hypochondriac—the 22-year-old man with a "heart attack," for example, or the middle-aged woman with "prostate trouble." These patients are examined, carefully reassured, and then served a restraining order if they refuse to leave the office.

In contrast, physicians live in fear of the medically sophisticated patient, who arrives on a stretcher complaining about a disease the doctor has never heard of. Such patients become neurotically obsessed with exceedingly rare diseases, partly because their chances of actually having what they are worried about are automatically slim, but also because considerable time and effort will be expended before the disease can be ruled out and they too are evicted from the waiting room.

A physician can look at a chest X ray and be fairly sure within seconds that you don't have lung cancer. But tell him that you might have *bangungut,* also known as "nightmare syndrome" (victims go to bed, thrash, cough, and cannot be resuscitated), because your father, grandfather, and two brothers all died of it. Then pass out in his office.

He will be quite careful before dismissing you as a "crock." If you are lucky, the whole process may involve so many examinations and tests that a real disease might turn up before it gets too far.

Not surprisingly, doctors try to keep the lay public from finding out about these really weird diseases. It's perfectly okay for *Lou Grant* to raise people's consciousness about jogger's knee, but no doctor will ever advise the networks on a script about familial periodic paralysis. The working theory is that an ounce of prevention is worth a pound of cure, and what they don't know won't hurt them.

We doctors know that *they* know that there's a lot more out there to fear than fear itself. There's Lassa Fever, for example, descriptions of which have until now been suppressed by the Nigerian Bureau of Tourism and Infectious Disease. We realize that harm can come from informing patients of the existence of such illnesses, but sometimes it just sort of slips out. Plus, we've been offered a lot of money. Thus we present ten diseases that—no kidding—you were better off not knowing about.

Most of these syndromes will make it difficult to find roommates but easy to find seats on crowded buses. Some put the worry back into being close. A few offer the advantage of removing your capacity to appreciate fully your situation. All have three features in common:

1. They are rare.
2. They are real.
3. They begin with innocuous, everyday symptoms.

Orzechowski's Syndrome

When Orzechowski's syndrome was first described in 1913, theologians could have taken this rare disorder as proof that God loves a good Polish joke. After all, why else would He create such a ridiculous disease as an afterthought to the common cold? Congress may make legislation this way, but He ought to know better.

This disease actually begins with a viral illness indistinguishable from an ordinary head cold. After a few days, the "cold" clears up, and the virus appears beaten. Field Marshal Rommel often used this same tactic to great effect in North Africa during World War II.

A few days later, however, the virus puts in an encore appearance. You develop a headache, and a fever, and from there it's all downhill. Your day becomes punctuated by sudden attacks in which your eyeballs abruptly start to flutter from side to side. The mildest of visual stimuli set off these spells. Simply shifting your gaze or blinking can trigger several attacks a day, each lasting minutes to hours. Crossing your eyes is really asking for it. The result is chaos for your vision, unless you are driving in Boston, where it may actually help.

Fortunately, those you meet may not notice your eyes. They will be too busy staring at the rest of your body, which will be providing a visual explanation of how this disease got its nickname—Dancing Hands/Dancing Feet syndrome. Responding to some primeval rhythm, torsos twitch and limbs flail during these spells. Sitting next to Orzechowski patients on subways can be brutal, and it's usually safest simply to hand over your wallet without trying to resist.

The mere sight of a patient with Orzechowski's syndrome makes children cry and dogs howl, but, oddly enough, the victims themselves are almost indifferent to it, perhaps due to the underlying viral inflammation of the brain. Orzechowski himself noted that most sufferers do not seem to be bothered by their rather absurd appearance, and cited that as useful in making the diagnosis.

The rest of the world feels quite differently, however. While these symptoms almost always disappear within a few weeks, by then you've been dropped by your entire social circle. We tell patients who *are* upset about the effect they create to move to New York for the duration of their illness so as to be less conspicuous. They can rent a small room on the Upper West Side and mingle with the crowd at the United Nations or the Mudd Club until respectable society is ready to take them back.

Ascher's Syndrome

Ascher's syndrome—perhaps better known as Double Lip Disease—was first described by the German physician K. W. Ascher in 1920, in an article called *"Blepharochalasia mit Struma und Doppellippe."* This disease remains a mystery to most physicians, who are still waiting for the film version. Nevertheless, experts see Ascher's as the best chance most Americans have of looking like a movie star. Unfortunately, that movie star is Rodney Dangerfield.

Ascher's starts with a little swelling around the eyes and lips—nothing new to survivors of boxing matches and bachelor parties. *This* puffiness, however, is caused by lymphocytes—white blood cells that ordinarily are key parts of your body's defense against infections. For reasons known only to themselves, thousands of these cells turn on the patient and start migrating from the blood to the eyes and lips for the express purpose of destroying all the elastic fibers there—the little strands that provide shape and resiliency to your face. Lose them, and you lose forever the chance to work for Nancy Reagan.

As they are attacked, the lips and gums become inflamed, swell to several times their original size, and finally give the appearance of double or triple lips. At this point, whistling will produce a Bronx cheer, and you may have to give up your trumpet lessons. Chapped lips may require hospitalization. The tissue around the eyes then becomes so loose and baggy that your eyes slide down into your cheeks. Eventually, your face resembles an Albanian village in a mudslide.

Partly because all lab tests are normal in Ascher's syndrome, and partly because there is no cure, doctors tend to delay before making the correct diagnosis. They will argue that your parents looked that way *too* when they were your age. Do not be stalled by such tactics. At the first sign of sag, find yourself a good plastic surgeon—one who thinks he can turn silly putty into dignified putty.

Familial Periodic Paralysis

Familial periodic paralysis is one of those rare disorders in which the name actually conveys meaningful information about the disease instead of the doctors who discovered it. Medical historians cannot completely explain this phenomenon, but apparently the illness was recognized around the turn of the century—after the birth of neurology as a specialty, but before neurologists fully understood the art of self-promotion.

As advertised, this disease runs in families and is characterized by recurrent episodes in which the patient simply cannot move. Of course, there are plenty of exceptions. Some victims have no recognizable family history; others never have a second attack, because, well, they don't do so well during the first.

The typical patient is under thirty when he has his initial spell, but is nonetheless able to live out a normal lifespan—although much of it is spent horizontal. The attacks begin with a sense of heaviness in the legs. This heaviness soon gives way to genuine weakness, which ascends inch by inch. Surprisingly quickly, victims find themselves completely paralyzed from the neck down. The weakness peaks in about an hour and clears over a day, usually with no long-lasting effects. If, for example, you happen to be lying on a beach when an attack comes on, the worst that can happen will be a bad case of sunburn. The brain itself is unaffected. Thus, if you're close enough to the water, you'll have plenty of time to worry about the decline of liberalism as you watch the tide come in.

Abortive attacks, consisting of stiffness and a reluctance to move, can be the first signs of illness. Precocious children often cite this disease as an explanation of why they cannot answer their mothers while watching television.

To figure out which children are lying and to detect impending attacks of your own, we urge you to recognize the "prodrome," or warning signs, that precede spells. Excessive thirst or hunger, sleepiness, irritability, or sweatiness can all presage an attack. Any of these tipoffs send some of our patients to bed until the danger period has passed, whether they have the disease or not.

Exactly what causes this paralysis is not clear, though some biochemical disturbance seems involved. Most patients improve with potassium supplements, but beyond that doctors can only advise avoiding the precipitating factors described by other victims. The most common of these are alcohol, excitement, exposure to cold, and menstruation. Given this warning, physicians feel, further attacks are the patient's fault.

Ondine's Curse

ONDINE: *Live, Hans. You too will forget.*
HANS: *Live! It's easy to say. If at least I could work up a little interest in living, but I'm too tired to make the effort. Since you left me, Ondine, all the things my body once did by itself, it does now only by special order. . . . It's an exhausting piece of management I've undertaken. I have to supervise five senses, two hundred bones, a thousand muscles. A single moment of inattention and I forget to breathe. He died, they will say, because it was a nuisance to breathe. . . .*

—From Act III, Ondine *by Jean Giraudoux*

Long before *Dallas*, long before Lucrezia Borgia, there was Ondine—a sea nymph from early German mythology who could have taught Charles Bronson a thing or two about getting even. She loved, and was then betrayed, by her mortal husband, a knight named Hans. The punishment for his infidelity was severe—Ondine took all automatic bodily functions from him. When her lover finally fell asleep, it was for keeps.

Fantasy, right? Well, take a deep breath (*inhale*), try to imagine how Hans felt, and read on (*exhale*). Sometimes, expiration imitates art.

In 1956 (*inhale*), three patients turned up in San Francisco with a strange problem, even for California (*exhale*). All three breathed normally on command (*inhale*), but, like Hans, if not reminded they forgot to breathe (*exhale*). In each case (*inhale*), difficulties had developed slowly after normal youths (*exhale*). Two had seizures while they slept (*inhale*) because of their oxygen deficit (*exhale*). By the time they consulted doctors (*inhale*), they needed respirators to assist their breathing every night (*exhale*).

Since then (*inhale*), more than forty similar cases have been found, and the syndrome has been named Ondine's Curse (*exhale*). Patients are 20 to 65 years old (*inhale*) and first complain of headache, shortness of breath, and decreased endurance (*exhale*). In several cases (*inhale*), autopsies showed damage of unknown cause to the brain's breathing center (*exhale*).

Fortunately (*inhale*), severe cases of Ondine's Curse are rare (*exhale*). In fact (*inhale*), doctors consider the disease's main danger the chance that people will read about it (*exhale*), become very conscious of their breathing, (*inhale*), and panic (*inhale*), because they aren't sure (*inhale*) that they will be able to breathe (*inhale*) if they stop thinking about it. (*INHALE.*)

Lassa Fever

Among the worries unique to our times, count Lassa fever. In the good old days, this virus was confined to West Africa, where no one went except by accident. Now it can pop up anywhere, thanks to air travel. And when it does, doctors agree, it's bad.

How bad is Lassa fever? It is so bad, it makes spending one's entire life in Buffalo look good. It is worse than detergent commercials. It is one of the most lethal and contagious diseases known to man. It is so bad that if you walk into a doctor's office and tell him that you have Lassa fever, he will not touch you, come close, or bother you in any way while you rifle the medicine cabinet or play with his stethoscope.

Such is the fear aroused by Lassa fever since its discovery a decade ago. Ironically, it begins like most other viral syndromes, with fever, malaise, muscle aches, and a sore throat. Similarity to a cold ends there, however, as the virus then moves through the entire body and persuades virtually every organ to close shop. Thus this disease is known for two distinguishing features—its high mortality and startling ability to spread from one person to another.

Take, for example, the first described outbreak of Lassa fever, as recorded by four Columbia University researchers. Experts in infectious diseases, they were studying viral infections in West African missionaries in 1969. That was how they heard about the case of L. W.

L. W. was an elderly nurse working in a missionary hospital in the remote town of Lassa, located in the Cameroon foothills of Nigeria. On January 12, 1969, she complained of a backache. The next day, she developed a sore throat; on the following day, she was unable to swallow. Unresponsive to antibiotics, she was flown in desperation to a larger hospital in Jos, Nigeria, on January 25. She died the next day.

A sequence emerged. The next three patients to contract Lassa fever were nurses who had cared for the preceding patient. The first two had died after developing backaches and symptoms resembling a cold. The third was transferred to the Presbyterian Hospital in New York City, the nearest good hospital.

News of her impending admission inspired many of the staff physicians to volunteer for tours of duty in Vietnam, which has no direct bus service from Nigeria. When she arrived in New York, the nurse with Lassa fever was immediately placed in full isolation—the medical equivalent of a Baggie—to protect those who tended her around the clock. Despite running temperatures as high as 107 degrees, she survived—although reportedly someone grabbed her handbag. Her recovery took months.

Meanwhile, Lassa fever maintained its dance of death. One of the researchers traveled to Nigeria to study the cases that continued to turn up. On February 18, 1970, four weeks after her paper describing the outbreak was accepted for publication, she died of Lassa fever in Jos, the first outbreak's final victim.

Needless to say, this epidemic created quite a stir in the medical community. For years, many nervous doctors considered the disease so dangerous that they refused to say its name out loud or move their lips while reading about it. A few extremists continue to examine patients with backaches only if the patients wear paper bags over their heads. The only positive aspect about all this is that it's pretty easy to book hotel rooms in Lassa on short notice. And if they do happen to be full, vacancies usually develop by the time you arrive.

Fortunately, most readers in this country have almost no chance of catching Lassa fever as long as they do not live within a hundred miles of a city with an international airport.

Steele-Richardson-Olszewski Syndrome

Steele-Richardson-Olszewski syndrome (SRO) is one of a large number of degenerative neurological disorders to which a simple diagnostic test can be applied—if you can remember the name and spell it correctly without peeking, then you probably don't have the disease.

Like most of these syndromes, SRO begins in middle age or later, and then progresses relentlessly as the brain is replaced by packing material. Victims eventually become demented, move with great reluctance and unsteadiness, and have difficulty in speaking clearly. Unless you are a senator, these problems usually force an early retirement.

Among these disorders, SRO is unique for its initial symptom, the inability to look down—an unbearable deficit to residents of the East Side of New York. Early on, victims of this disease lose strength in the muscles that turn the eyeballs down. This deficiency in downward gaze progresses slowly at first and may not be immediately noticed. Only in retrospect does the patient remember that the first ominous sign was tripping on a curb, or stumbling on the stairs, or spilling a little food on his tie.

Eventually, the body becomes inflexible, and the soul applies for a transfer. Complications set in, and everyone calls it a day.

Now, no one is saying you have SRO just because a few peas rolled off your fork at dinner tonight. Then again, no one is saying you don't. It's just too soon to tell.

The Cinderella Syndrome

There's more than one Cinderella syndrome in medicine, and none involve Grace Kelly, or even Helen Gurley Brown. The oddest is a skin condition known as *erythema dyschromicum perstans,* which may not help you meet a prince but could get you into *People* magazine anyway. After all, how many folks have skin that makes them walking Rorschach tests?

This rare disease begins as a small gray patch the hue of burnt newspaper under the eyes or on the arms. The spot slowly enlarges into an irregular ring, as other patches, in varying shades of gray, pop up elsewhere. These blotches shift around and merge with each other, forming bizarre patterns. It's sort of like having a movie-map showing the growth of the Third Reich projected on your chest, only this time Germany wins.

The patches are caused by your own white blood cells, the body's soldiers that are ordinarily assigned the job of gobbling up invading bacteria. In the Cinderella syndrome, though, the white cells act like sailors on leave after six months at sea. They abandon the blood vessels and roar into the skin, where they eat melanin, the pigment granules that give color to the skin.

Having done one foolish thing, the engorged, gaily hued cells don't know what to do next, so they wander aimlessly under the skin, creating wavy lines as they move. These migrations offer one small hope to victims—if they don't like the way they look this week, there's always the chance they'll be happier the next.

The rash doesn't respond to any known treatment, though sometimes it disappears on its own when the white blood cells decide to face the music and go home. Until then, patients must put up with the good and bad of having shifting ink blots on their faces and bodies. On one hand, previously affectionate people turn on you as your mottled visage begins to remind them of some primal childhood terror. On the other, you'll never have trouble getting into discos again.

Lethal Midline Granuloma

Lethal midline granuloma is a rare inflammatory disease of unexplained nature that is every bit as bad as it sounds, maybe worse. It is so unpleasant that we'd rather not go into details other than to warn you that the first symptom is a runny nose. As for what happens next to your face, let's just say that it is important to be sure that the damage isn't really due to tuberculosis, leprosy, or end-stage syphilis—all diseases that you'd rather have than lethal midline granuloma.

Beyond that, we just don't feel like discussing it, okay?

Cobalt Beer Syndrome

You've seen the commercials. It's the end of another long day of punching cows. A herd of horses with tall men on them stampede the local saloon. The next scene shows one or two cowpokes inside, exchanging admiring glances with a beer-bearing beauty.

Where are the other cowboys? If they've made a lot of these commercials, they could have cobalt beer syndrome, in which case it's going to take them a long time to get from the corral to the bar. With swollen legs and decaying hearts, they may find that just getting out of the saddle could consume most of Happy Hour.

The syndrome was born over twenty years ago, when beer manufacturers discovered that cobalt enhanced the flavor of beer. Local brewers, particularly in the West, began to add cobalt in liberal doses to their special brews. The result was a quick victory for free enterprise in its periodic range wars with public health.

After several years of grabbing for all the gusto and cobalt you can get, the gusto settles at your waistline, while the cobalt settles in your heart—where the muscle fibers swell and die. As the heart weakens, blood backs up in the veins like water behind a dam. The increased pressure causes swelling—first of the legs, then of the belly and scrotum. (This process explains the distinctive walk of many cowboys.)

Poor oxygen uptake by the slowly circulating blood turns the cowboy a dusky blue. He also becomes kind of slow-talkin', because not so much blood gets uphill to his brain anymore. What does is full of the buffalo chips usually cleaned up by his liver, which is also in the process of checking out for the last roundup.

Doctors only recognized this syndrome in the 1960s, and eventually, beer manufacturers were persuaded to take the cobalt out of their secret formulas. Still, cobalt is an occasional pollutant in the water used to make beer, and God knows what they've added to take its place. So happy trails, stranger, and when you're having more than one, make it a Shirley Temple.

Prader Willi Syndrome

It's one a.m. on a Saturday night, and you're standing in the dim glow of a refrigerator's light bulb. You want something to eat, partly because you are hungry, but mostly because you are starving for love, because you thirst for spiritual nourishment, because that girl went to Colorado and never came back. All this thinking only makes you hungrier. You pop some lasagne in the oven, and you open another beer.

An hour later, the last *Mary Tyler Moore* rerun is over, and the lasagne is gone. Only the top got warm. You lie in bed, in that expanding trough in your mattress, understanding that you've done it again. You've eaten too much, far more than you wanted. Your pajamas feel tight, and you have trouble getting comfortable. The bedspread seems heavier than you remember, and you're vaguely short of breath. Your stomach blocks the view of your feet, and your chin blocks the view of your stomach. You feel fat. Fat, fat, fat.

In the final analysis, there are only two possible explanations for your sudden identification with beached whales. Some earn fatness; others have it thrust upon them. If your idea of a double date is to take a Sara Lee cake to the movies, you are in the former category, along with most of the people who eat a little more than is good for them. If you eat the cake, the foil wrapping, and the cardboard top, however, you may be one of the guiltless inhabitants of the second—victims of a tragic and incompletely understood disease. You may have Prader Willi syndrome.

The bearers of this uncommon, inherited disorder are *really* fat. Some unknown neurological defect drives them to eat—anytime, anyplace, anything. For them, it's one a.m. on Saturday night all year long, and the entire world with all its riches is a big refrigerator.

The Prader Willi literature is full of stories of one-man supermarket sweeps. For example, one child regularly ate several loaves of bread directly from the freezer, or two entire cakes at a sitting. By the age of five, he had already had his stomach pumped many times at hospitals after swallowing a variety of noxious substances, including DDT, fruit pits, and detergents.

Some victims have been caught stealing food, rifling garbage cans, and eating animal food after chasing their pets away. Others have been known to eat entire jars of mayonnaise or sticks of butter. One boy helped his class bake a dozen apple pies as a school project. At recess, he sneaked back in and ate eight of them.

On intelligence tests, most Prader Willi victims are a little slow. They also tend to be short, and to have poor muscle tone and underdeveloped genitals. What separates them from the rest of us is that they are almost always extraordinarily pleasant people.

That these diseases exist at all demands reflection on the nature of the universe and our place in it. You could conclude that any system that can come up with syndromes like these has no ultimate purpose; that life, as Hobbes put it, is nasty, British, and short. Conversely, you may reason that the existence of such bizarre disorders stands as proof that there is a higher order of intelligence, a Supreme Being with an ultimate plan to which we are not privy. We would agree, though we would add that if a Divine Providence truly created these diseases, He is not only pretty smart, but also really pissed off.

Life-Threatening Infections You Can Catch From Your Pets

I had a dog, his name was Blue,
Bet you five dollars he was a good dog, too.
—Deservedly Anon. Folk Song

Right. And *we'll* bet you ten dollars that Blue, if given the opportunity, would have turned his master in to the police for a plane ticket to the Caribbean and the companionship of a saucy French poodle. And we'll give you odds.

We've made a lot of money this way, because most Americans live in a fantasy world when it comes to their pets. They see life as an endless loop of Lassie reruns. They thought Checkers was enough to redeem Richard Nixon, just as they once warmed to Ronald Reagan because of his horses. They ignore the dark side to our dealings with pets, the reasons we sometimes call them "animals."

We don't want to overstate the danger, or imply that we think pets are intrinsically evil. After all, they're not so smart; in the final analysis, a dog is a dog, and a horse is a horse.[1] But, as physicians, we also

---

[1] Of course, of course.

know that every interaction between Man and The Beast That Does Tricks, Sometimes, is like playing in traffic. Animals harbor a variety of parasites that can turn your organs into diet cola, rob you of your intellect, and put the rest of you in a medical doggy bag. Look what hanging around with the Budweiser horses did to Ed McMahon, and what owning the New York Yankees did to George Steinbrenner. No wonder, then, that most of our patients have been wary of their pets since childhood. Usually they trace their fears to seeing the Disney classic *Old Yeller*—a traumatic childhood experience that stands with birth, puberty, and the divorce of one's parents as a pivotal event in an American's maturation.

In case you've repressed the memory, Old Yeller was a dog who gave up pieces of his tattered yellow hide in reckless endeavors like fighting grizzly bears. His courage was exceeded only by his ability to absorb punishment—indeed, he has been the inspiration for countless white boxers.

These tactics quickly removed our hero from the ranks of All Things Bright and Beautiful, and turned him from Young Yeller to Old Yeller by the age of two, which is like being 14 years old for a human being, according to the theory of relativity. Though he was not pretty and not very bright, Yeller's fierce loyalty nevertheless won him a place in a pioneer family, not to mention our hearts. (Yeller was a bit of a pioneer himself. He was the first "ugly" dog to make it big anywhere but the living room rug, shattering the show-dog mold of Lassie and Rin Tin Tin. In his day, he was the Barbra Streisand of the Disney kennels.)

The rest is history. A rabid wolf attacked the family. Old Yeller fought it off, absorbing his usual beating and contracting rabies with it. Since veterinarians had not yet invented the after-dinner speech, the family's son had to put him to sleep by shooting him with something resembling a bazooka. Several times, as we recall, though perhaps it was only the report of a single shot that has echoed in our memories for years.

As boy and dog stared at each other along the barrel of the gun, all parties had a better understanding of the word "ambivalence." The boy was learning that sometimes you have to give up the things you love most, and occasionally that means shooting them. Old Yeller, who had quickly considered all avenues of escape and saw that it was hopeless, realized that he should have bitten the hand that fed him while he could. As for us—the 11-year-olds in the audience who would always consider Old Yeller far more deserving of our tears than Ali MacGraw at her best—we were awash with emotions. We were wondering what kind of man Walt Disney was to let this happen. We were asking our parents why doctors couldn't cure rabies with a pill or something. And, above all, we were thinking about that big dog down the street that had been drooling on our sneakers, and we were wondering what would happen to us if *we* got rabies.

Thus we learned that pets bring many things into our lives, and that some of them are fatal diseases. If the rest of the country only knew the story. Despite *Old Yeller,* there is still one dog for every six Americans, and they account for many of the more than 150 diseases that people catch from animals.

Of course, lots of these diseases are minor skin infections, like puppy dog dermatitis. This infestation by *Sarcoptes scabiei* produces an intensely itchy scaling rash that your internist will poke at with a Q-tip while breathing through his mouth before packing you off for the dermatologist. These illnesses usually respond to treatments that fall far short of actually shooting the dog.

But other infections carried by dogs, cats, fish, and birds can render your body less appealing than a bowl of partially eaten Meow Mix left out in the rain. If Americans knew about these, they would confront veterinarians and SPCA officials, and ask, "Whose side are you on?"

A selection follows.

Cat Scratch Disease

Cat scratch disease is a prototype for these illnesses in two key ways:

1. You feel terrible once the illness has set in.
2. The animal feels perfectly fine.

In fact, the cat is not ill at all. It is only carrying a virus on its paws. This virus will not infect the cat, but *will* slip inside you when kitty takes a playful slash at your face as you try to put the catnip away. A week or so later, lymph nodes in your armpits, neck, and groin swell up and start to drain pus, at which point your lover may become a bit suspicious about where those scratches really came from.

The lumps themselves are not hazardous. If left alone, the swollen nodes and the washed-out feeling that accompanies them leave with hardly a trace, much like your lover. The main danger is that they will be mistaken for lymphomas or other tumors requiring surgery. Many patients have had "cancers" removed by a surgeon, only to find that their lumps were just another form of kitty litter. While recovering from surgery, patients often ask what kind of landfill cats make, and whether German shepherds can be taught to climb trees.

Although we deplore this sudden hostility toward cats, we are not really surprised by it. After all, people who own cats are usually a little weird. Deprived of ordinary human friendships, they put all their emotional eggs into the single basket of their relationships with their cats. And yet they are the first to reach for a strychnine-filled mouse when the cat opens up an artery, or curls up on their face as they sleep.

It's not the cat's fault—his brain is just the size of a pistachio, so how much mischief can he deliberately make? He just wants attention. Thus a little patience and a few simple rules will allow you and your cat to grow old together, free of parasites and unwanted visits from relatives or old friends.

First, don't let your pet have too much responsibility too soon. Pushing it to grow up will only make it grow up too fast, when it can't handle it. Exert some control over your cat's television habits. Be especially sure the set is off when you are both eating your dinners, even if you use separate cans—this is family time. Don't overburden your cat with your adult problems. All too often, people use their pets as therapists or confidants, forgetting a single important fact—a cat is really dumb. He doesn't understand what you are saying. He doesn't want to hear about your neuroses; he wants to claw up the couch.

If none of these suggestions work, and your cat continues to show signs of hostility, we suggest:

1. Getting out the lead booties and enrolling him in swimming classes down at the Y.
2. Taking him out for "dinner" at a Chinese restaurant. It will be the meal of his life.

Salmonellosis

In 1975, the Food and Drug Administration banned interstate trafficking in pet turtles. What did this mean? True, the FBI had fallen on hard times—embarrassed by Watergate, overwhelmed by the narcotics industry, it needed some easier assignments to recoup its reputation. But still, your average pet-store owner is a far cry from Dillinger, and photographs of G-men posing beside confiscated turtles failed to capture the nation's imagination. An official attempt to have turtles classified as a dangerous, mind-altering substance failed, despite the tragic discovery of an Ohio congressman dead, slumped over a bowl of turtles.

There was actually good reason for the ban: more than half of the pet turtles in the United States are carriers of *Salmonella* bacteria, which cause two million cases of gastroenteritis in this country per year, equal to the entire export total of Central America and Argentina combined. Many patients have fifty or more bowel movements per day, far exceeding EPA guidelines. Very young or old patients often become so dehydrated that they pass out; some cases are even fatal. Countless others merely wish they were dead, but are forced to endure two weeks of misery before recovering.

The ban on pet turtles caused a seventy-seven percent decline in *Salmonella* infections from turtle-associated strains of the bug, but the disease remains common because so many other animals carry the bacteria. About twelve percent of cats are infected, as well as twenty percent of dogs. *Salmonella* is also common among the chicks and ducklings many children find in their Easter baskets. These cuddly balls of fluff realize that they have only a few weeks to live, and the bacteria represent their best hope of taking a child or two with them.

We personally do not believe that the best way to protect ourselves from pets carrying *Salmonella* is to ban the pets. If you outlaw ducklings, soon only outlaws will have ducklings. Stiffer penalties and stricter enforcement of those penalties ought to convince an Easter chick not to give innocent children diarrhea. And if he can't get the message, he'll have plenty of time in the pen to think about it.

Bubonic Plague

Examining what the cat dragged in has long been a ritual in American life. Many potential doctors lost interest in anatomy while poking a stick at the remains of a field mouse left on the doormat.[2] Disgust, though, was usually tempered by admiration for an animal that slept on windowsills most of the day, lived off the land at night, and could get away with almost anything via the excuse of being in heat.

We would have felt a little differently had we realized that the cat might be bringing home bubonic plague, better known as "the Black Death."

Which Black Death, you ask? The same Black Death that has been attributed to everything from heresy to halitosis; that swept the world in the sixth century, the fourteenth century, and, to a lesser extent, at the end of the nineteenth century; that has frightened and inspired authors from Dionysius to Camus; that most doctors refer to as *The Plague*—*that* Black Death is alive and well and living in California.

In fact, bubonic plague never really disappeared. Cases have appeared sporadically for years, though most have been too mild to be reported. In 1980, however, a 47-year-old California woman noticed that her cat was coughing and having nosebleeds. Four days later, the woman developed similar symptoms. Within days, she was the first plague fatality in the United States since 1924.

Today, doctors understand that the disease is caused—not by religious indiscretion or forgetting to floss your teeth—but by bacteria

---

[2]Many families mistakenly interpret this gesture as a form of tribute. Actually, anthropologists believe that it is just a convenience, the evolutionary forerunner of leaving your books on the kitchen table when you come home from school or throwing your clothes on the only chair in the bedroom.

called *Yersinia pestis.* This bug is carried by fleas and frequently attacks small animals, especially rats, squirrels, rabbits, and chipmunks. Thus it is firmly entrenched among these creatures in the American West.

Contact with these animals leads to infection in an occasional Boy Scout or nature lover. They make their beds; they can lie in them. But, at the edge of town, these fleas also attack "city mice" and pets, eventually bringing the Black Death to normal people minding their own business. Although antibiotics can curb cases if used early enough, and vaccines make another major epidemic unlikely, sporadic cases will almost surely continue to pop up. Thus, a few common-sense precautions seem in order:

1. Never pet a rat without boiling it first.

2. Never kiss a squirrel on the lips.

3. Wear a flea collar around the house or to any setting where you are likely to encounter other living things.

4. Always remember that a rabbit is not a toy. It is a shy, graceful creature that would like to see you swell up and die.

Babesiosis

Suddenly, being chic is chic again. Rich people are feeling good about themselves. They aren't ashamed of having a lot of money, or having spent time at prep school, or owning people. They're proud of their portfolios, and, if they have babesiosis, they tell the world about it.

Babesiosis, you see, is the plague of people who are rich enough to take their pets on vacation with them. It is a disease of the elite—and why not? Other people have *their* diseases—sickle-cell anemia, for example. In contrast, babesiosis isn't even something you can inherit. Most cases have been caught in one very special place: Nantucket, the exclusive resort island off Cape Cod, which is home to many famous writers and at least one breed of tick, *Ixodes dammini.* These ticks carry the *Babesia* parasite; both are picked up by Packy after a romp in the woods, and he carries them home to Master as a way of teaching *him* how to play dead. Shortly after the tick bites, the parasites set up housekeeping in your red blood cells. The resulting illness can take you from the Social Register to a *New York Times* obituary with a photo in a matter of weeks.

When you have babesiosis, you look as pale and drawn as a *Vogue* model. Your blood count falls, while your body is wracked by fever, chills, muscle aches, and nausea. The sense of fullness in your belly means that your spleen has swelled to fight the infection. Patients often complain of a sense of weltschmerz, but we suspect that it is affected.

Ironically, the earliest recorded victims of babesiosis were beasts of burden—Chapter 9, Verse 3 of Exodus describes a divine plague of cattle and pets in Egypt that probably was a form of this disease. Today, however, its victims are definitely of a better class.

So if your name is Buffy or Chip (or if you just wish it were), monitor yourself carefully when you return from vacation. If you feel tired and have been running a temperature, if you've been having drenching sweats or aching muscles, you might have babesiosis. If you do, there's one way to keep the glow of your fading tan alive: tell your friends about it. Throw up on the floor. Finally, drop the news that your spleen is enlarging.

They'll die of jealousy.

By the way, there's no treatment.

Toxoplasmosis

Toxoplasma gondii is not an obscure Indian pacifist; it is a parasite that lives in about half of us, and it is yet another reason to distrust cats. This bug is carried around by domestic felines, as well as cougars, bobcats, and Asian leopards. Cats excrete the parasite's eggs everywhere: into the soil, the water, the living room rug. From there, the eggs are picked up by all kinds of animals, including rugby players.

Thus about ten percent of the lamb and a quarter of the pork sold in this country contain the eggs. If these meats are eaten while under-cooked, toxoplasmosis follows.

Inside the body, the eggs hatch and grow into a form called the *trophozoite*. The *trophozoite* is as cute as a button and will go any-where in the body to play, although its favorite haunt is the lymph glands, which upon infection swell into hard lumps. Most infections are mild, with only one or two lumps and associated symptoms like fatigue, malaise, headache, and mild abdominal pains—about what one experiences during an income tax audit. But occasionally the germ spreads everywhere, and your body gets so lumpy that it resem-bles a rosary. That's just what you may need when the germ invades the heart, lungs, and particularly the membrane that covers the brain, which may eventually have to be shipped to Lourdes under separate cover.

There are a few simple precautions that you can take to ensure safety from *Toxoplasma gondii:*

1. Get rid of your Asian leopard immediately. Just untie it, and let it go. It will soon become someone else's problem.
2. Cook all meat, particularly cat meat, until it is black in the middle. Serve plain, or on a bed of wild rice.
3. Thoroughly wash and then bury all garden-grown vegetables without eating them.
4. Clean kitty litter boxes with napalm or some other government-approved bleach.

The picture we have painted is a grim one. And we have not even mentioned psittacosis, a pneumonia caught from birds, and the most difficult disease in medicine to pronounce without spitting; tularemia, a systemic illness carried by rabbits; or the self-explanatory toxacara viscera larva migrans. Still, we feel that the capacity of your pet to transform you from a taxpayer into a deduction on someone else's 1040 does not demand a tough attitude toward all animals.

No doubt some animals deserve it. Roy Rogers stuffed and mounted Bullet and Trigger for offenses that Rona Barrett could only hint at. But recent statistics out of New York City (where else?) suggest that our relationships with pets may be less dangerous than associations with other human beings.

Dog bites were down 16.7 percent in 1980 in comparison with the previous year, for example. The number of incidents of humans biting other humans increased 24 percent over the same period. In fact, bites from every species except humans declined.

Examination of the data reveals even more depressing trends. Individuals in the 20-to-25-year-old group received the most human bites; right behind them were the 15-to-20-to-year-olds. That college-age and high-school-age individuals should lead the pack in getting bitten says something sad about the quality of education in this country. No wonder Johnny can't read; he can't even keep his hand out of someone else's mouth.

Even more dispiriting is the finding that while half of the bites were classified as "aggressive," almost 40 percent of the bites were attributed to "unknown" activities. These people cannot recall how they came to be chewed, yet we are considering drafting them into our armed forces.

Most disturbing in this mournful litany was the finding that 5 percent of all human bites were caused by children biting their doctors. We recommend that such children receive a radical medical therapy administered by trained specialists. Its technical name is "The Old Yeller Treatment."

Physical Fitness Is Hazardous to Your Health

I'm not feeling so good.
—Alberto Salazar,
after winning the
1982 Boston Marathon

American culture thrives on the marriage of ideas. Still, we are more than a little puzzled by the current confusion of perspiration with recreation. We understand the joys of competition. Even for us, the thrill of victory has its allure. But the agony of the feet—and virtually everything else—is another matter, usually medical. We've taken care of too many javelin wounds to ignore the obvious: Physical fitness is hazardous to your health. Few things in life are as dangerous as good clean fun.

Thus we were especially concerned a year or so ago when both *Time* and *Newsweek* ran cover stories on the fitness boom, transforming it from a mere trend to a bona fide fad. It recalled for us the horror of the early 1960s. That turbulent decade witnessed the birth of fifty-mile walks, folk dancing, and the first outbreak of jogging, which spread rapidly despite intensive aerial spraying of runners. There was an upsurge in active sports like swimming, touch football, and running for President, accompanied by the decline of more cerebral pastimes like Monopoly, pinball, and locking your sister in the closet. Abdomens were flat. Spirits were flatter. It had to stop.

Just in time, God provided *ABC's Wide World of Sports.* Some of you may be unfamiliar with this institution because you have been living in a cave in Tibet. But for many of us who grew up in the 1960s, that world was all we had. It wasn't much, but it was better than watching golf,[1] and sometimes almost as satisfying as a World War II movie. It dangled boxing as bait, balancing our love for violence against our wish to inflict it upon Howard Cosell. The fight was always the last segment of the show—those TV people aren't fools, you know. But with that small promise before them, millions of Americans put away their baseball bats and ax handles, and sat through "highlights" of horse shows and auto races with names like the Firecracker 500 or the Hasidic Open. And they loved it, so much that they made *Wide World of Sports* the most popular sports show in America.

The genius was partly in the packaging. But even more important was ABC's insight that American men were tired of winning, of losing, and—above all—of sweating themselves. They wanted a graceful way out. They wanted an excuse to sit inside, where it was cool, where they could pretend it was Miller Time all day long, while retaining their self-images as good old boys who loved their sports.

Thus, as the other networks caught on, weekend television came to be filled with imitations of *ABC's Wide World of Sports.* And today, when there are no real athletic events to cover, we are fed sports spinoffs, like "NFL Cheerleaders Tag Team Mud Wrestling" and "Leroy Neiman at Home."

An overjoyed America became a nation of spectators.

In general, doctors were delighted with this trend toward armchair (as opposed to wheelchair) quarterbacking, despite the costs. True, business fell off for orthopedic surgeons, and psychiatrists began to

---

[1]What isn't?

diagnose strange new psychoses.[2] Irreparable damage was done to the English language by people called "baseball players." Phrases like "he came to play" or "running through pain" were tossed around as if they actually meant something. But, all things considered, Americans seemed safer sitting in front of their television sets than running around a field like goats.[3]

Unfortunately, though, *watching* sports may be an idea whose time has come and gone. Physical fitness itself is back with a vengeance— and the evidence can be found in emergency rooms everywhere. Rather than watching sports and commercials at home, Americans are once again outside, killing themselves in their attempts to live longer. When they do go shopping, they are apt to buy Japanese running shoes instead of American beer, thus worsening the national trade deficit.

Doctors regard all this activity with a bloodshot eye. Most physicians simply don't like sports. They are still bitter about being stuck in right field back in Little League, which at that level of play is like being appointed ambassador to Nepal—little responsibility but less fun, and no one notices you until you screw up. Besides, professional restrictions and vehicular safety codes require doctors to use golf carts in those rare situations in which a Mercedes is inappropriate, like picking up the newspaper on the front lawn.

We'll admit that there are some benefits to the running boom—for example, more young women are wearing sleeveless T-shirts and thin cotton shorts in public than at any time during the Eisenhower Administration. (Our female colleagues report a similar epidemic of scantily clad young men.) But as physicians, we can see people without *any* clothes on *whenever we want!* So most of us have stuck by our old

---

[2]See Anna Freud's classic analysis *The Bear Man* (Viking, 1962), about a football coach who actually answered to the name of an animal.

[3]These conclusions were drawn before physicians understood the radiation involved in watching television. See Chapter 4 in *That's Incurable! Vol. II* (Viking: in press).

hobbies, like building tax shelters in bottles. Those doctors who do indulge in sports choose those in which there are heavy odds that they will not be the ones who get hurt—hunting, for example. All other athletic activity is considered dangerous.

Thus we feel obligated to let the American public know just how dangerous fitness can be. You don't need the Surgeon General to tell you about the obvious hazards involved in some sports. Everyone knows about sky diver's earache and the nosebleeds that plague mountain climbers. But you *do* need this book to tell you about the subtle, rare, and all-too-real complications of modern life in general— and sports in particular—that have recently appeared in the medical literature. The columns of *The New England Journal of Medicine* and other publications are overflowing with horror stories about activities that once seemed safe. A sampling follows.

The Case Against Running

The earliest case report demonstrating the hazards of running comes down to us from the Persian Wars. In 490 B.C., in the wake of the Athenian victory over the army of Datis at Marathon, a Greek runner named Pheidippides was dispatched with news of the triumph. He reached Athens but never got to the postscript. Still, in his final act, he did communicate an even more important message—running can make you drop dead.

Since then, a variety of subtler complications have been described by physicians in an attempt to dissuade their patients from running themselves into the ground, so to speak. For example, we have cautioned our patients that the common practice among marathoners of dabbing benzene-containing rubber cement on their feet to cushion blisters can cause anemia, or even leukemia. They were undeterred, until we pointed out that having leukemia could hurt their running times. Virtually all our other warnings have been ignored, strengthening our suspicion that the runner's brain suffers thousands of tiny concussions as he bounces along.

Otherwise, many would have given up the "sport" after hearing of "Penile Frostbite: An Unforeseen Hazard of Jogging," as reported by Dr. Melvin Hershkowitz of Jersey City in *The New England Journal of Medicine* of January 20, 1977.

Dr. Hershkowitz described the case of a physician who went out for a routine thirty-minute run in mid-December. The temperature was 18 degrees Fahrenheit; the wind-chill factor made it seem even colder. Five minutes before the end of the run, the physician noted "an unpleasant painful burning sensation at the penile tip . . . the pain increasing with each stride."

On examining himself at home, the physician was horrified to discover early frostbite of the penis. Fortunately, rapid therapy produced a complete cure. Federal laws prohibit us from providing details of either treatment or response, though a videotape is available to special customers.

Almost as frightening is jogger's nipple—a painful breast abrasion produced by repeated rubbing against a shirt, usually the runner's own. Only a few years ago, this syndrome was distressingly common among serious women runners. For example, fifteen percent of the runners in the 1976 Women's National Marathon in Minneapolis reported "chafing."

Since then, most women runners have learned to prevent such problems with petroleum jelly or protective shields we doctors call "pasties." Thus most current victims of this syndrome are male. In one recent Mayor Daley Marathon in Chicago, twenty runners were treated for painful or bleeding nipples. Nineteen were men. His Honor would have appreciated the irony.

Men and women alike are subject to the indignities of the gastrointestinal complications of running, as reviewed by Dr. Stephen N. Sullivan of Victoria Hospital, Ontario, Canada, in *The New England Journal of Medicine* in 1981. He surveyed fifty-seven long-distance runners and found plenty of evidence that the legs aren't the only part of the anatomy in movement. Among his findings:

—10 percent reported heartburn when running.

—30 percent occasionally or frequently had the urge or need to defecate, often forcing what he called "a nip into the bushes."

—a quarter had cramps or diarrhea after competitive running. "Only six percent had severe nausea or retching," he added!

Only?

Our response, as members of a profession devoted to avoiding pain as much as relieving it, is a question. If God had meant us to run, why did He give us the El Dorado?

Waterskier's Enema

On the surface, waterskiing seems the perfect sport of physicians. For starters, you have to be rich to play it. Just as important, it doesn't demand much teamwork. In fact, it doesn't take much more than staying on your feet, hanging on, and pretending you're not bored by going around in circles. These tasks should pose no problem for anyone in private practice.

But, as with most endeavors in which taking off one's glasses is recommended, there are hidden dangers. Drowning, for one. Shark attack, for another. In more crowded waterways, where speedboats crisscross like waterbugs, there is also the constant threat of PT-109 syndrome, in which the victim is run down by a Japanese destroyer.

Add to these the risk of waterskier's enema and waterskier's douche, both commonly seen in beginners. In these syndromes, water is forced under high pressure into all sorts of nooks and crannies when the patient-to-be falls at high speed, or is towed in a sitting position. At best, such a tumble can leave you with an incredibly clean acromphalus.

The more ominous sequelae were reviewed in the *Annals of Emergency Medicine* in 1980 by Dr. Kenneth W. Kizer of Hawaii. He summarized cases of lacerations, infections, and general disruption of the delicate plumbing down there, all due to falls during waterskiing. Complications included miscarriage, infertility, and bleeding requiring surgery, sometimes on the driver of the boat.

Thus, as physicians, we recommend that anyone who either has a womb or has spent time in one avoid waterskiing faster than five miles per hour. Even safer, try standing on your waterskis in your bathtub, gripping your soap-on-a-rope firmly with both hands (no hot dogging!), and making *vroom-vroom* noises with your mouth. In either case, you're safe as long as you don't fall.

SAFETY WATERSKIING

The Vicious Cycle

You can look it up.

In the last ten years, there has been a dramatic increase in the number of Americans riding ten-speed bicycles. Over the same period, there has also been a steady increase in the number of Americans dying from cancer.

Coincidence? Perhaps. But perhaps not. At this point, physicians are ready to blame almost anything on bicycles—and with good reason. In recent years, several new neurological and urological complaints have been discovered among riders, syndromes that give new meaning to the expression "the vicious cycle."

One of the first of these diseases was dubbed cyclist's palsy by Dr. Thomas A. Converse of Minneapolis, Minnesota, a cyclist himself. In a 1979 report to *The New England Journal of Medicine,* he described "an insidious onset of numbness, weakness, and loss of coordination in both hands," a constellation that soon left him unable to hold a pen. His illness turned out to be due to pressure from the handlebars on his palms, leading to compression of the ulnar nerves—actually, a common problem among cyclists. Fortunately, this condition is responsive to several months of riding around in the back of a limousine.

Since then, several other syndromes have tried to claim the title "cyclist's palsy" for themselves. Most are blamed on the narrow hard banana seat on these ten-speeders—what urologists call "hell on wheels." These seats have been found to cause inability to start urinating, inability to stop urinating, inflammation of the prostate, and torsion (twisting a full 360 degrees) of the testes.[4]

One 46-year-old man described in a 1981 *New England Journal* report lost all sensation in his penis for one month after a bicycle trip, though he retained the capacity to become aroused and have inter-

---

[4]Contrary to popular belief, enduring testicular torsion does not separate the men from the boys. Indeed, it tends to turn the former into the latter.

course. In short, he was able to have sex; he just couldn't enjoy it. There's a philosophical lesson in that story somewhere, and we hope we never learn it.

The Playing Fields of Eton

There will always be an England—at least if the British heed the warnings of Dr. J. B. Bourke, a surgeon from Nottingham. Reprinted here in its entirety is his letter from the February 10, 1979, issue of the premier English medical journal *The Lancet:*

Gum Chewing at Cricket

Sirs,—*The Observer* of Jan 28 reported details of the injury to the Australian batsman Darling on the first day of the fifth test match in Adelaide. Darling was hit under the heart by an ordinary ball from Willis, collapsed, choked on his chewing gum, and somehow swallowed his tongue. When the crisis of choking was over, the injury to Darling was found not to be serious.

Over the past two to three summers whilst watching first-class cricket, I have noticed an increasing number of players chewing. On the second day of the Trent Bridge test match, at the beginning of the New Zealand innings, an urgent signal was sent to the England dressing-room, and eventually the twelfth man brought out a packet of chewing gum which was quickly distributed among several players. During the two New Zealand innings, most England players were chewing, and some replenished their gum, returning the tell-tale silver paper to their pockets. Subsequent inquiry revealed that chewing gum whilst playing first-class cricket is a common habit.

Chewing gum, inspired whilst playing cricket or other sports, may become lodged in one of the bronchi and cause wheezing or infection. If it gets stuck in the trachea, asphyxia and sudden death may ensue. The cricketer will be at greatest risk when he takes a sudden inspiration—as when hit in the abdomen or chest whilst batting (as in Darling's case) or when reaching for a high catch.

I am unaware of any catastrophe resulting from the use of gum by cricketers, but it is fortunate that skilled attention was immediately available for Darling—it will not be at most cricket matches. It would be prudent for cricketers to abandon this apparently widespread habit, and we must hope that youngsters will not follow the dangerous example now being set by English and Australian test cricketers.

J. B. Bourke

Scrum Pox

Like cricket, rugby is traditionally an English sport, but it has always had a loyal following among American men too chicken to play real football. In recent years, though, the sport has enjoyed a mild surge in popularity—students at Harvard currently rank it somewhere above ROTC in terms of coolness, albeit still considerably below drug addiction. It's easy to see why.

For the uninitiated: the game involves rolling around in the mud with a bunch of sweaty men wearing unattractive shirts. You spend a good part of your time catching your breath, recovering from stunning blows, or yelling strategies to teammates, like "look out!" There is one offensive play: kick the ball. There is one defensive play: protect the groin. At the game's end, you drink more beer than you really want, sing vulgar songs, and throw up. Then you apply for business school.

It's not all glamour, though, as demonstrated by the current epidemic in England of scrum pox.

This syndrome is not a disease per se; it is a blanket term for skin infections transmitted during the face-to-face contact of pileups. According to a recent report in the *British Medical Journal,* the problem is limited to "forwards"—rugby's version of football's linemen. But among those players, the problem is severe. One hospital team had seven cases among fifteen players in a recent season. A gentleman's agreement prevents these players from competing, but before big matches, this agreement and other vestiges of civilization are routinely forgotten.

For years, the cause of scrum pox was obscure. Some thought it was a form of another skin disease associated with athletes, known commonly as jock itch. But, even for rugby players, this notion was disgusting. Recently, microbiologists have isolated several different bacteria and viruses as the guilty agents. The most common of these may be a form of herpes virus that has been variably called *Herpes gladiatorum* or *Herpes venatorum.* (Latin: *venator,* sportsman. Impressed?)

This disclosure merely strengthens our conviction that rugby is a sport to be avoided. If one must get herpes, we can think of a better way. Still, this new data has spawned a variety of recommendations on how to avoid scrum pox if you insist on spending your afternoons with those big, sweaty boys:

1. Never wear tight or suggestive clothing.
2. As long as the ball is in play, wear rubber gloves and pants.
3. Avoid pileups, and stay away from the ball.
4. Stop washing your rugby outfit. If there is inadvertent physical contact in the game, it won't be repeated.
5. After the game, never drink another player's beer. You don't know where his mustache has been.

Slot-Machine Tendinitis

Physicians near casinos have long known of slot-machine tendinitis—inflammation of the right shoulder resulting from repeated yanking of the one-armed bandits' arms. According to a report in *The New England Journal of Medicine* of May 28, 1981, steroid injections may help, though the best treatment remains rest or an early jackpot. If these fail, we recommend attacking the machine with a crowbar. In any case, if you play long enough so that you hurt in the shoulder before the wallet, we don't have much sympathy for you.

That same issue of *The New England Journal* described a related syndrome, Space Invader's wrist. This disorder represents a strain of the ligaments used in the rapid, repetitive arm movements involved in playing the popular video game. It's a fine example of technology changing our lives for the better.

Urban Cowboy Rhabdomyolysis and Other Dangers of Dance

Disco and punk rock may well be the most important cultural developments in this country since the Smile Button, but, from a medical perspective, they are choreographed demolition derbies.

How else can one feel after learning of "New Wave subconjunctival hemorrhage?" As recently described in *The New England Journal*, this syndrome consists of bleeding in the whites of the eyes after doing the

Pogo—a dance that involves little more and nothing less than jumping up and down for hours. Nor do we have much sympathy for the victims of disco felon—a hand infection resulting from repeated snapping of the fingers. Finally, there's the dread urban cowboy rhabdomyolysis—massive destruction of muscles from riding mechanical bulls.

Of course, not all injuries are so exotic, as shown in a "Survey of Roller Disco Dance Injuries" by Dr. Matthew Corcoran of St. Columcille's Hospital, Dublin, published in 1980 in the *Journal of the Irish Medical Association.* After a roller disco ballroom opened near his hospital in 1979, he kept track of all injuries treated in his emergency room that could be connected to this new form of dancing.

Over a one-month period, the casualty list included twenty-eight victims. Half of them had broken bones, most commonly the wrist. Three required hospitalization and general anesthesia. The other patients were treated for lacerations and/or blunt trauma, and sent home.

By comparison, Belfast seemed safe.

The list goes on and on. We haven't the time or space to go into diseases like the short leg syndrome—an orthopedic disaster resulting from running in only one direction on a banked track. Its once-vigorous victims are consigned to a lifetime of Walter Brennan imitations.

Suffice it to say that sports physicians are working around the clock—well, several hours a week, anyway—to understand the physiology of complaints like tennis eye, in which a well-hit tennis ball traveling at more than fifty miles per hour can cause serious damage to your eye, or sports sunburn.

What you do with this data is your business; only later does it become ours. In the meantime, we will try to be compassionate, though it is difficult to empathize with many patients, especially the runners. While we have heard of the concept of running through pain, we cannot understand why anyone would want to do such a thing. Running *away* from pain makes so much more sense. Thus we advise that when playing any sport, keep constant vigilance for any sign of discomfort. When pain appears on the horizon, stop immediately, and take a taxi home. Examine yourself. Mix yourself a drink. And turn on *ABC's Wide World of Sports.*

How to Recognize Your Own Psychiatric Emergencies

"Doctor, am I going crazy?"

This question, so often unspoken, dominates many of the encounters between patient and physician. All too often, the patient goes home with his doubts unresolved, skeptical that his doctor might be interested in his mental health, and thus reluctant to raise the issue.

Not necessary! True, most doctors consider mental illness an ugly business and spend a good part of their day hoping the topic won't come up. But, when dealing with the anxious patient, the physician is usually groping for a way to broach the subject himself.

Even when the doctor does not directly pose the question, he may offer subtle signs that it has crossed his mind—the arched eyebrow, for example, or sudden snorts of laughter. He may leave his stethoscope in his pocket throughout the exam. Or he may not examine you at all, instead writing a Valium prescription after only a few minutes, murmuring something about "medicine for your muscle spasms."

What can this mean? Are you really crazy after all?

Experts agree that, more often than not, the answer is yes.

For proof, psychiatrists cite the famous "Midtown Study," on the prevalence of psychological disorders in midtown Manhattan. Psychiatrists felt that 81.5 percent of those surveyed were "less than well," while 23.4 percent were considered "impaired." True, the era was the 1960s, and all the participants lived within walking distance of Bloomingdale's. Taking these factors into account, we estimate the actual "impaired" rate to be no more than 5 percent in the general population. Among our readers, of course, the figure is closer to 87 or 88 percent.

So what to do? After all those doctor bills, who can afford nine years of analysis, even if there's always the chance that you might turn out like Jill Clayburgh?

The solution is self-treatment, using time-honored (and relatively cheap) outlets such as compulsive overeating, knuckle-cracking, and stuttering. One-on-one psychotherapy should be reserved for those times when all hope is lost anyway.

Of course, successful self-treatment demands the ability to recognize these crises when they are finally upon you. Which brings us to the point of this chapter—how to recognize your own psychiatric emergencies.

Now you may read parts of this chapter and think you recognize yourself. Do not panic. If you suddenly realize that your constipation is consistent with psychotic depression, there's little to be gained tonight by looking in the Yellow Pages under "Shock Treatments."

Go to the refrigerator. Take a bite out of everything in sight. Then read on.

You may have something much worse.

Depression

Everyone has periods when they are overcome by sadness or sensations of helplessness and insecurity. These feelings are not normal.

They add up to the syndrome of depression—what we doctors call "the blues." Clinically, this syndrome can range from mild adjustment reactions, such as often follow the death of a loved one, to severe psychotic breaks, like those routinely seen in Latin America after the home team loses in soccer.

There are several drugs useful in treating depression, but experts agree that the safest and most effective treatment for many patients is electroconvulsive therapy—better known as shock treatment. Unfortunately, we cannot treat every American in need of a good dose of blue bolts, given our national energy problems and our current quest for independence from Arab oil. For example, the electricity demands of Boston alone after the annual Red Sox collapse would require the construction of two new nuclear reactors. As is, even those lucky few sick enough to get treatment receive only a fraction of the voltage we would like to give them.

The problem, then, is figuring out just where on the spectrum of depression you lie, and how badly you need treatment.

Mildly depressed people are usually acutely aware of their loneliness. They solicit aid from friends and look for magical solutions to their problems. They frequently imagine that regaining a lost love or winning an idealized new one will instantly reverse their fortunes. A fine portrayal of a mildly depressed man was offered by actor Robert DeNiro as the homicidal Vietnam veteran in *Taxi Driver*.

In cases of severe depression, people often give up. They do not look to their friends for hope or relief. They are sure that others cannot or will not help them, and that things will never improve. Unfortunately, they are usually right.

In the event that you do not recognize these symptoms in yourself, don't give up. You may be suffering from a case of masked depression, in which the patient protects himself from feelings of sadness by simply denying that they exist. Although masked depression can be confusing to the diagnostician, other clues are usually available, and good psychiatrists can recognize them, gain insight into the patient's defenses, and tear them apart. Gradually, the patient learns just how

MILD DEPRESSION

profoundly depressed he really is. Occasionally this insight is the deciding factor in an unconscious weighing of suicide's merits.

For example, depressed people commonly manifest their absorption in themselves with unusual concern for their physical health. They may be certain that they have a cancer or fatal infection—a punishment that, at some level, they are certain they deserve. They wander from doctor to doctor in search of confirmation. If you know people like this, you should immediately buy them this book.

In recent years, however, as appreciation of the complex interactions between body and mind has increased, depression has been shown to be associated with actual physiological changes. Doctors use these clues to diagnose depression, and so can you. For example, the metabolic rate of depressed patients slows down, and many gain weight. Alternatively, appetite may decrease, and they lose weight. Some patients cannot fall asleep; others sleep constantly. Another common complaint is constipation, though early depression can be marked by diarrhea.

This description should eliminate confusion from the mind of any rational person.

Anxiety Attacks

Anxiety attacks are common, relatively minor psychiatric emergencies, which are often characterized by the sudden onset of shortness of breath, a feeling of tightness in the chest, nausea, a cold sweat, and a tingling sensation around the mouth and fingertips.

These spells are especially important because they must be differentiated from heart attacks, which often begin with shortness of breath, chest tightness, nausea, a cold sweat, and an unusual sensation in the arms and jaw.

One quick way to make the distinction yourself is to breathe into a paper bag. (Never use a plastic bag. As every mother knows, if you even look at a plastic dry-cleaner's bag when alone in a room, it will wrap itself around your face and suffocate you.)

If you are having an anxiety attack, rebreathing your own carbon dioxide will correct a blood disturbance that is increasing your drive to breathe. The sensation of shortness of breath will pass, and the attack will break. Burt Reynolds used this technique in the movie *Starting Over,* and twenty minutes later he was in bed with Candice Bergen.

Of course, if you are having a myocardial infarction, your heart needs every atom of oxygen it can get, and breathing into any kind of bag could kill you.

If you do go to an emergency room, we suggest going to one where you are not yet well known, or, perhaps, wearing a simple disguise. This single precaution will give a true heart attack a fighting chance of getting diagnosed. By considering the history, the examination, the electrocardiogram, and the results of some blood tests, the doctor will decide which diagnosis is correct. And if you are having an anxiety attack, he will reassure you, tell you to get some rest, and give you some Valium.

In contrast, if you are having a heart attack, you will receive the most advanced care medicine can provide. You will be rushed into a coronary care unit, a great many blood samples will be drawn, and rather large needles will be stuck into your arms or some even less convenient part of your anatomy. You will be hooked up to a cardiac monitor while being examined by several doctors, and perhaps even a medical student.

Then you will be reassured, told to rest in bed, and, to keep you as calm as possible, you will probably get some Valium.

Dementia

"Doctor, am I demented?"

In offices across America, physicians face this half-question, half-plea over and over every day—occasionally several times within fifteen minutes from the same patient. Usually there has been trouble at home. Maybe the patient has heard his children joke about his "toys in the attic." Perhaps he has noticed that in little ways he is slipping. Some days he may wake up in the closet. Others he may get to the bathroom and forget why he went there. Before long, the demented patient says little and does even less—all to avoid embarrassment, until he can confront his doctor for the answer.

We have a simple way of dealing with this question. We pretend we didn't hear it. If, after a few minutes, the patient appears to have forgotten the question, we say, "yes." Since the patient doesn't know what we are referring to, no one's feelings are hurt.

For these unfortunate folks, dementia becomes a way of life. To doctors, though, dementia is a distinct clinical syndrome. Usually it is irreversible; many cases are due to arteries getting plugged up by cholesterol plaques—the penalty of a lifetime of baconburgers and Lucky Strikes. As blood flow to the brain slows to a trickle, the neurons decide to pack up and call it a career.

Other people have an inherited tendency to suffer the premature death of brain cells. Researchers do not fully understand how this damage occurs, nor can they state the likelihood that any given person will become prematurely senile. Still, if your father began to laugh aimlessly or chew on his tie while still in his fifties, you'd best get your affairs in order now.

There are, however, a small percentage of cases in which a treatable cause can be found. Among these causes are thyroid disease, infections like syphilis, and nutritional disorders such as pellagra and vitamin B-12 deficiency. Thus, it is important for the physician and the patient to remember that dementia means disease, and to recognize its early signs.

No sign is as important as memory impairment. Demented patients are fully alert and often have excellent long-term memory—that is, they can remember details of their childhoods with startling clarity. However, they are unable to make or retain new short-term memories. For example, they have trouble with the names of new people and places. They may even forget things they have just heard or read!

Many patients first note dementia when they have difficulty with calculations. They may be unable to understand how much money they owe the grocer, or how much change to expect. To cover themselves, they simply hand the clerk a twenty-dollar bill and accept whatever is returned. This strategy has never endeared old people to newspaper vendors, and, as inflation runs wild, it is becoming less effective.

Other patients initially notice the cardinal complaint of dementia—memory impairment. Demented patients are fully alert and often have excellent long-term memory—that is, they can remember details of their childhoods with startling clarity. However, they are unable to make or retain new short-term memories. For example, they have trouble with the names of new people and places. They may even forget things they have just heard or read!

Another serious problem for the demented is handling abstract ideas and broad philosophical concepts. They are often forced to retreat to safer ground, rigidly holding to familiar slogans like Hegel's postulate that reason is the conscious certainty of all reality. Meanwhile, they are tinting their hair blue in order to keep it from turning yellow.

All these problems become more severe when compounded by the most common manifestation of dementia—memory impairment. Demented patients are fully alert and often have excellent long-term memory—that is, they can remember details of their childhoods with startling clarity. However, they are unable to make or retain new short-term memories. For example, they have trouble with the names of new people and places. They may even forget things they have just heard or read!

Naturally, these deficits force demented people to retreat from society. Ironically, the rate at which dementia progresses accelerates when someone loses his social function, such as his job, or loses physical capabilities. In their isolation, many of the demented develop paranoid notions about others and even their own bodies. For these unfortunate folks, too, this book would make a wonderful gift for Christmas, or just an unexpected surprise.

Last but not least among the many features of dementia is memory impairment.

Remembering what has been forgotten is, of course, technically impossible, as pointed out by thinkers from Plato to Gracie Allen. After all, if something can be remembered, then it wasn't forgotten in the first place, was it, George? Thus many of you may have difficulty making the correct self-diagnosis.

One quick test is to ask yourself whether reading this section gave you a headache. If the answer to that question is no, then the answer to the question posed at the outset—whatever it was—is yes.

There are several remedies to the problem, none wholly satisfactory. If you are in an occupation such as politics, you can go on for some time before being discovered and appointed ambassador to Spain. Jobs demanding more skill, such as being shot out of a cannon at the circus, may require major adjustments in your life.

One approach you might enjoy is leaving your spouse, taking up with someone younger than your children, and leaving him or her all your money. If that doesn't turn things around, we recommend going to discos to remind yourself that, bad as life is, there are others who are much worse off. In any case, there's no point in fighting. Go with the flow, knowing that at last you can say or do anything you want without anyone raising an eyebrow.

Neuroses

Patients constantly ask us whether we think they are neurotic. Usually we are successful in stifling retorts like, "Is the Pope Catholic?" Stealing a line from our psychiatric colleagues, we come back with, "Why do you ask?" Not as clever, perhaps, but it does let them talk.

Through this technique, we have learned that the most crippling neurosis among the postwar generation is the one we call the fat-child syndrome. This syndrome is epidemic among those born in an era of peace, prosperity, and—above all—plenty. Raised on butter instead of guns, they thought being worldly meant eating French toast and turkey pot pie.

Not surprisingly, a lot of them got fat. Today, many have slimmed down, but remain scarred psychologically by too many trips to the husky boy's department at clothing stores. They are left with a disturbance of body image reminiscent of schizophrenia. Even when not on a diet, they feel that they are breaking one. Guilt and fat have been internalized.

Answering a few quick questions can help you assess whether you are neurotic about your weight and suffer from the fat-child syndrome:

1. When you were a child, and your parents offered to buy you a pet, did you ask for a dog but secretly want a tapeworm?

2. Do you weigh yourself:
   a. Every day.
   b. Naked.
   c. After going to the bathroom.
   d. After running several miles, and letting the sweat dry.
   e. All of the above.

3. Do you despise your skinny brother who weighs himself once a year, fully dressed, holding a book, without even emptying his pockets, in public places like drugstores?

4. Is your wardrobe devoid of horizontal stripes, because back in 1962, your mother told you that horizontal stripes made you look even fatter?

5. When people tell you that they can't believe you were ever fat, because you look so thin now, is your reaction to distrust them?

6. Do you still get nervous when you look at the ads for camps for overweight children in the back of *The New York Times Magazine?*

If the answer to any of these questions was yes, probably the answer to all of them was yes. Doctors are very sympathetic to victims of the fat-child syndrome, since it is so common among physicians themselves. When we were kids and our friends were out playing ball, we were inside getting smart and eating chocolate chip cookies.

As is true for most neuroses, there is no cure for the fat-child syndrome. We recommend staying away from rich desserts and rugby shirts, and not bringing any progeny into this world.

Paranoia

Being paranoid isn't as much fun as it seems from the outside. After all, paranoid people are loners. They collect injustices. They never forget minor slights. They get inappropriately angry waiting in line, in heavy traffic, or when jostled in a crowd. They take it very personally when they get arrested.

Paranoids are constantly looking for hidden meanings and secret motives in any gesture. A minor incident can remind them at a sub-conscious level of some vulnerability apparent only to themselves, and they will respond with wild rage in an attempt to compensate. These rage attacks are normal, and even useful when driving in the city, but they can poison human interactions such as business negotiations or getting second dates.

Thus, we are especially pleased to reveal that a treatment for para-noia finally exists. This medical breakthrough can eradicate any irra-tional fears lurking in your soul and put you at peace with the world. But we are not going to provide you with any details because we want to hurt you.

Obsessive Compulsive

The obsessive patient, who often appears to be so effective with the details of daily life, is in reality caught up in a continual conflict between obedience and defiance. The question he is constantly asking himself is, "Shall I be good, or shall I be naughty?" What distinguishes him from the rest of us is that he briefly considers being good.

The roots of this conflict generally lie in the early power struggle between parent and child, a struggle that often focuses on bowel habits—specifically, toilet training. Some psychiatrists feel that early toilet training—say, before the age of two—may push a child toward an obsessive personality, while letting the child find his own way in and out of the water closet favors a more normal development. Other experts say that those psychiatrists have been paid off by the manufac-turers of Pampers and rubber sheets.

Regardless, they *do* agree that life is a joyless endeavor for these patients. They tend to be preoccupied with dirt, time, and money, as well as squeezing up their toothpaste from the bottom of the tube. Answering a few quick questions can help you decide whether you are among them:

1. Did you get upset when you learned that the sun is a middle-aged star?
2. Do you worry about the effect of continental drift on property values?
3. Is your idea of a good time flossing your teeth?
4. When Faye Dunaway was scrubbing the floor in *Mommie Dearest,* did you get into it? (Be honest.)
5. It's eleven o'clock. Do you know where your children are?

If the answer to any of these questions was "yes," then you are an obsessive compulsive. The prognosis is grim. You will probably never know the emotional intimacy of a close relationship. If you think you have had one in the past, think again—it wasn't so great, was it?

But don't worry—you can have something even better. Head for the nearest medical school and make your way to the admissions office. Offer your neatly typed name in application. You may never be truly happy, but it sounds like you will make a terrific doctor.

Schizophrenia

Schizophrenia is the most complex of psychiatric disorders, and if you were expecting us to straighten out the mess here, you have made the common error of confusing our book with *An Elementary Textbook of Psychoanalysis* by Charles Brenner, M.D. Too late now. Let's just say that schizophrenia involves much more than "split personalities." And if you feel that there are eighteen people inside you, and three or four are stable enough to hold down a decent job, you've gotten off easy.

For schizophrenia is a disturbance of several areas of psychological functioning. Many patients have trouble defining their "ego boundaries"—they can't tell where they end and another person begins. Thus the schizophrenic cannot tell if thoughts are yours or his. If someone else speaks, he cannot be sure he did not do the talking. Sometimes, he cannot even tell whether an arm or leg belongs to him or someone else. It's like being in a Japanese subway all day long.

Not surprisingly, the schizophrenic patient has difficulty organizing his thoughts by the usual rules of logic. The border between illusion and reality is lost. Words or gestures take on unintended meanings, often sexual or paranoid. Notions of which the schizophrenic is ashamed take on the form of disembodied voices.

As a convenient test to determine whether you are an evolving schizophrenic, we have prepared the following set of questions. What have you got to lose in answering them? It's already been a long night. Turn the light on and respond in a firm yes or no. Equivocation will result in government surveillance.

1. Do you hear voices in airports?

2. Do you really think that if you put a quarter in that machine you will be able to get a newspaper out?

3. When Ronald Reagan fell asleep during his audience with the Pope, did you agree with his press secretary that the President was only pretending to doze to see if the Pope would try anything?

4. Do you believe that if a dog sleeps on his back, he's gay?

5. Do you own a Walkman?

If the answers to any of these is yes, you are an impending schizophrenic. You should feel lucky to be an American. As a schizophrenic, you will become eligible to buy a gun through the mail and do anything you want.

Though the material in this chapter has covered the principal disorders of mood and thought, we realize that, like many tracts written by physicians for the layman, it skirts key issues. Rather than deal with the concrete problems of everyday life, it falls back on what is known in the trade as psychiatric mumbo-jumbo. The reader may not understand how this data is relevant to his or her life.

In short, it's not dirty enough.

Do not despair. For now, and only now, you are prepared for the thorniest difficulties in the life of the anxious—an area of medicine so closely bound with psychiatric emergencies that usually the most the doctor can do is try to figure out which came first. We are speaking, of course, of the subject of the next chapter—sexual dysfunction.

The Hypochondriac's Guide to Sexual Dysfunction

In recent years, sex has made its way out of the locker room and into the doctor's office. Everyone agrees that the shower floors are a lot less slippery as a result, but medicine has been complicated immeasurably. Nevertheless, most doctors would concede that the transition was inevitable, if painful. After all, sex is not a game—it is an incurable disease, or at least the most powerful invitation to human suffering we know of outside of medical school. Hippocrates himself thought that sex might one day be a medical concern, and he warned doctors to be ready. "Sooner or later," he said, "this whole mess is going to fall into our laps."

And he was right. Today, sex is the doctor's problem. The change was more sociological than medical. The sexual revolution, which began so innocently a generation ago with the television show *Leave It to Beaver,* eventually swept the country, even destabilizing parts of Canada. It produced radical changes in values. Sexual fulfillment became the name of the game, the toast of the town, the heart of the darkness.

Unfortunately, you could put all the sexually fulfilled people in America under the clock at the Biltmore and still have room for the Lithuanian Air Force Band. Which brings us to the point of this chapter—as revolutions go, this one produced more than its share of casualties. Our offices are filled with the walking wounded. Much of our time is spent trying to figure out which among them can be saved.

Despite this huge need, most doctors remain deliberately aloof on the whole issue. This apparent indifference should not be taken as evidence of a true lack of interest or compassion; rather it reflects the discomfort produced by questions in this area in most physicians, a discomfort that is often accompanied by mild nausea, fainting spells, and nosebleeds. Thus doctors will go to extremes to keep the topic from even coming up. Many of our colleagues will only see a patient if his mother or priest is present. Some set off their beepers and leave the room as soon as the subject is broached. Others immediately send patients off for expensive tests—the more invasive, the better.

Some insight into the making of a physician can clear up this mystery. By the time they are born, most doctors are too old for sex as we know it. At each step of his education, the doctor responds to the calls of unbridled passion by making safe, sublimating detours, maintaining a professional calm to avoid scuffing his loafers. As a premed student in college, the doctor deduces the linkage of sex and death by causing fatal allergic reactions in guinea pigs, which can turn blue and still maintain erections (it's not as easy as it looks). As a young, tired intern, he gets slapped around by nurses who have received formal training in fogging his glasses and shortening his stethescope with a minimum of wasted motion. Finally, after years of sacrifice and the establishment of a successful practice, the mature physician can experience the ultimate sensual thrill of squeezing a Mercedes into a tight parking spot, followed by hitting a golf ball cleanly while surrounded by people of the same color. No wonder he's not anxious to have the subject of sex come up.

Although patients, in contrast, begin life with more natural attitudes, in the course of growing up and cultivating mature relationships, they, too, lose their childlike innocence and become alienated from the normal expression of sexual desires. The smallest of traumas can pull the plug of the sexual bathtub. A woman may suddenly feel unwanted when she sees her husband turn immediately to the bra section of the new Sears catalog. A man may discover that the secret words that arouse women are "American Express." Both sexes may feel unable to live up to the unrealistic, stereotypical expectations about sexual stamina and accomplishment that pervade our culture.

Thus, by the time the adult reaches our offices, he regards sex as a physical and emotional vacuum. Like nature, he abhors a vacuum, yet is concomitantly compelled to rush into it. As far as he is concerned, one's organs should never be seen and only occasionally heard from—the rare muttering from most tissues usually suggests to the active imagination imminent self-destruction. But the sexual organs are not like common everyday tissues. If inadequate attention is paid to them, they tend to generate their own publicity. If the patient tries to pretend that they don't exist, orifices that formerly dared not whisper their names soon refuse to stop shouting. In no time at all, the sexually dysfunctional patient can be rendered completely incapable of concentrating on the more important issues of life, like renewing one's driver's license or practicing a firm handshake.

Faced with a rebellious body and indifferent physicians, many patients try to ignore the rich animal and vegetable kingdoms that comprise the *ratatouille* that we call sex and which Freud termed "nooky." They wade upstream against the surging juices of their forebears, until every natural instinct is killed. The medical term for these unfortunates is "investment bankers."

As responsible physicians, we make clear to our patients that being able to lend money to New Jersey is nothing to be proud of. The stakes are clear. You will never meet David Susskind until you learn to go with your reproductive flow. You *must* confront your sexual needs with honesty and (if you are like most of our patients) with humility. Learn to recognize your sexual fears, no matter how bizarre. And if one of yours involves building a wooden box, you had better read the next section very carefully.

Koro

If a man walked into your office with his penis clamped inside a wooden box, what would you think? Being an ignorant layman, you would probably assume that this was another fund-raising campaign, and drop in a quarter. Since we are physicians, we wouldn't put any money in at all. We would know instantly that this man was a victim of Koro—one of the more curious manifestations of sexual gridlock.

This syndrome was first described by the British in Malaysia,[1] but has since been found throughout the world. A man with Koro syndrome suffers the delusion that his penis is shrinking, and that if it disappears inside his abdomen, he will die.[2] Those afflicted with this delusion usually adopt the solution of tying a ribbon around their reproductive organs, or, alternatively, encasing both kit and caboodle in a gaily decorated wooden box—a tactic we feel is especially hazardous to the caboodles. Such patients can develop subsequent medical problems, ranging from splinters, to fatigue secondary, to increased wind resistance.

Treatment of such patients can be very difficult. We used to try to reassure patients that if by chance the penis should disappear into the abdomen, they certainly wouldn't die. We generally found ourselves conceding, however, that they would be better off dead in this situation. As a result, they would go out and build bigger boxes and burglar-proof them. Our new approach has been simply to make sure that the box conforms to housing construction standards, and advise the patient to wear a tablecloth instead of shorts. After that, we let the chips fall where they may.

Couvade

Couvade is derived from a Basque word meaning to "sit upon eggs."[3] It is an extraordinarily common condition in which men develop the symptoms of pregnancy, often to their amazement.[4] Its victims are always the husbands of expectant mothers, men who develop one complaint after another, until they are suffering from severe morning sickness, headache, backache, and progressive abdominal swelling.

---

[1] Only recently has a team of Malaysian anthropologists been permitted to enter England. We await their findings with interest.

[2] The premise may be faulty, but you have to give them credit for the forceful logic of their conclusion.

[3] As far as we know, this is the only word ever derived from the Basque.

[4] Not to mention that of their mothers.

The pains of couvade have no basis in physical disease. They arise solely from hysterical imitation, from a psychological demand for equal time. Couvade has attained its full flowering in one African tribe in which, at the appropriate time, the husband takes to the only bed in the hut and starts complaining of labor pains. As the rest of the village, including the shaman or witch doctor, gathers around to help, sympathize, and soothe, the pregnant wife goes off into the woods and has the baby. She returns and kicks everyone out of the house and her husband out of bed, while the whole village rejoices to see him back on his feet.

This syndrome is also well known in the West. One recent study found evidence of couvade in nearly one-fourth of expectant fathers surveyed in Rochester, New York. The manifestations, though, are usually more subtle in this country. In our practice, an early clue that one of our patients is about to have a difficult few months is the discovery that he is wearing underpants with the logo "Baby Under Construction" stitched across the front. Such cases of couvade can be difficult to treat. Fortunately, they tend to resolve spontaneously in about nine months, unless the patient is a male elephant, in which case a cure can take up to two years.

A doctor confronted with such a patient can take the easy way out. He can deride him, make jokes about the rhythm method, give the patient a plastic dill pickle, and play a tape of Paul Anka singing "Havin' My Baby" over the waiting-room intercom as the patient leaves the office. Or the physician can do as we do, recognizing that this confused man is a patient who needs help like any other patient. We attempt to reassure the patient concerning his symptoms, prescribe extra vitamins, enroll him a breathing class, and charge the couple for two deliveries.

Pure Erotomania

We do not wish to imply that psychosexual disturbances are an exclusively male domain. Far from it. Take, for example, De Clarambault's syndrome, popularly known as pure erotomania. Most reports of this disorder come from the French and Italian literature,[5] but it is seen often enough in this country for physicians to realize that it is more than a psychiatric oxymoron—for many, it is a way of life.

The victims of this disease are usually but not always women. They become consumed with the delusion that someone is passionately in love with them. Their "lover" is generally a public figure who knows

---

[5]Where else?

the erotomaniac casually, if at all. Still, once the notion has taken root, it can dominate the lives of both.

Typically, the patient pursues her beloved relentlessly, waiting for the release of the passion she is sure is there. She follows him home, leaps out unexpectedly and embraces him in public, and sends sexually explicit singing telegrams to him at work. These tactics never worked for us in college and are no more successful in these situations.

The patient's own marriage and children are abandoned as she seeks the presence of her beloved. He in turn often has some explaining of his own to do to save *his* marriage, as women with pure erotomania have been known to force their way through windows into their quarry's home. The results can be fascinating family dinners. Children develop better eating habits because they can't bear to leave the table during such encounters.

We have treated several such patients after trying ineffectually to get them to transfer their affection to ourselves. Some of our cases are already described in the medical literature, but we cannot write about them here without compromising the sacred doctor-patient relationship and the confidentiality of the medical record. Instead, we can offer a composite case history:

A young woman, Miss D.,[6] fell hopelessly in love with a United States Senator while working in his office as an aide. Though quite pretty, she was socially his inferior. Unable to read or write, her only accomplishment had been winning a beauty contest sponsored in her forgettable small town by a leading manufacturer of flea collars. The Senator (H.), on the other hand, had been made an honorary Dallas Cowboy Cheerleader, and was one of a handful of presidential (R.) confidants who called Sec-

---

[6]Not her real name.

retary of State Shultz (S.) "George."[7] He was quite cool to her advances until she stumbled across some photographs while ironing old correspondence. Then they got married.

Within a short time, the Senator died after catching Lassa fever from a troop of Nigerian Girl Scouts (N.) flown over to take part in a ribbon-cutting ceremony. His wife inherited his vast fortune, including natural gas deposits located on his western ranch and beneath the back yard of their fashionable Washington (W.) home. She went on to become Vice-President of the United States, and now serves on the board of directors of one of America's most important hamburger chains.

This pathetic case history indicates just how persistent the delusory state can be. The cost in human lives and torn pantyhose is incalculable. Attempts at treatment can be very frustrating for the concerned practitioner, because of the duration and depth of the neurotic delusion. Ultimately hospitalization or confinement to Alabama may be necessary to prevent the patient from harrassing her "lover" or extracting her revenge.

Piblokto

Piblokto is not truly a disease of sexual dysfunction. It is included in this chapter because its victims are often mistaken for exhibitionists or pure erotomaniacs, and because we had nowhere else to put it. In truth, erotic thoughts are the furthest things from the minds of the unfortunate women who suffer from it.

Also known as the Arctic hysteria syndrome, Piblokto is an altered state of consciousness seen in Eskimo women who are fed up to their

---

[7]He also called President Reagan, Senator Strom Thurmond, and everyone else "George," but that's another disease for another chapter.

mukluks. They are tired of igloos, of huskies that can't be housebroken, of husbands who go out hunting and end up trapping and skinning Budweiser. For these women, being cold has lost its charm.

An otherwise trivial incident—such as being attacked by a wolf—can be the club that kills the baby seal. Once the Piblokto syndrome is triggered, the victim pulls off all her clothes and runs naked among the ice floes, screaming gibberish. (Gibberish, of course, shares certain linguistic qualities with the normal Eskimo language—an unfortunate coincidence that has caused more than one Eskimo Maidenform woman to be institutionalized.) The attack passes after one to three hours. Afterward, the patient is completely normal, except that she cannot remember the entire episode—in contrast with her neighbors, who usually can't forget.

Such attacks represent a rejection of the patient's situation in life. It is an extravagance allowing the patient to butter her bread on both sides in the nude. It permits the discharge of built-up emotional steam rather than turning it against oneself. The patient is, in fact, better able to maintain a normal life after the release of her hostility.

This syndrome is only rarely seen in the United States below the Arctic Circle, where television game shows provide a similar outlet for ritualistic discharge of aggression.

Priapism

Though our discussion thus far has emphasized the psychological, doctors know that when it comes to sexual dysfunction, there is more than one way to run over a dog. No matter what your analyst told you, there *is* a physical side to sex. Of course, disorders affecting the tools of the trade are inevitably less varied than the disturbances created by a fevered imagination. But, cruelly enough, they tend to affect men more than women, and have therefore received a lot of attention from both physicians and Rotarians. And perhaps the cruelest of them all is priapism.

Priapism refers to a persistent erection of the penis[8]—persistent to a troublesome degree. Contrary to popular myth, the name is not derived from General Nho Gho Priap, the Vietnamese explorer credited with discovering the prostate. Actually, it is named after the Roman god Priapus, who invented the concept of the service entrance.

This condition is almost always harmless, if embarrassing, but it can be due to tumors of the bladder or prostate. Although one might reasonably conclude that all adolescent males between 13 and 18 are in the process of being consumed by bladder growths, such problems are quite rare. It is usually a psychological disturbance that leads the patient up the slippery slope of priapism. These conditions are disgusting, and we refuse to discuss them further.

[8]Or limb, as it is referred to by our southern grandmothers.

Impotence

Physicians are rarely troubled by the emotionally debilitating, uncontrollable erections of priapism. There is less and less of that sort of thing as one moves up in years and tax brackets. Sexual arousal is considered to be a sign of poor breeding.

Impotence, in contrast, can lead to no breeding at all—an example of what William Blake called "fearful symmetry," and what one woman we know described as "a bummer." Which points out one of the most crippling features of this problem—like bad breath, impotence is usually called to your attention by someone else. Not surprisingly, the complications that follow all too often extend beyond the bedroom. With impotence comes the stigma of failure, a lack of vigor, an inability to make snap decisions, or a tendency to snap one's decisions too quickly.

The causes of this complex complaint are numerous, and they are reviewed every few weeks by the supermarket magazines. In most cases in which an etiology can be determined, the problem is psychological. Fear of failure, fear of women, fear of appearing vulnerable, fear of cutting yourself, and fear of your mother discovering those magazines top our list. Alternatively, you could have cancer or diabetes.

Even if you do, the greatest problem for you and other impotentates is understanding that impotence is not necessarily a problem at all. Your gun may be spiked for sound ecological reasons.

As scientists from Malthus to Fran Lebowitz have pointed out, our greatest long-range danger is too many people. Nature has devised many ways to control overpopulation among other species. If there are too many lemmings, they run into the sea and drown. If there are too many caterpillars, they eat all the leaves and die. If there are too many small, yappy dogs, the mayor or someone orders them rounded up and shot.

But nature has considerably more difficulty with human beings, especially the subpopulations that are the greatest drain in our resources—advertising executives and close presidential advisers. Humans don't like to swim out too far. They won't eat most leaves because of terrifying experiences with their mothers. Warfare was a good idea, but too nonselective. It tends to remove those most beneficial to society, as in the case of Ted Williams, who was plucked from the Red Sox outfield in 1942 after batting .356 that season and .406 the year before.

Impotence, though, is the alternative to war, the most conscientious of objections, and the most passive of resistances. It is a phenomenon unique to human beings.[9] It may be nature's way of letting us out of this mess with a whimper, not a bang.

Fatal and Near-Fatal Allergic Reactions to You-Know-What

The characters: you and the man of your dreams.

The place: your bed or his, it doesn't matter.

After an appropriate period—we recommend two to three minutes—you feel your heart beating faster, pounding against your chest. Your breathing becomes rapid and shallow; gasps and tiny strangling noises emerge from somewhere in the back of your throat. A tingling sensation spreads over your arms and legs. Your skin becomes pink, and then mottled. You feel your head throbbing; the room starts to spin.

You may be having an orgasm. Big deal. Alternatively, you could be having a severe allergic reaction to your lover's semen, and the next breath you take may be your last. It's tough to tell.

For years, doctors did not believe that this syndrome existed, and dismissed case reports with remarks like "what a way to go!" and small snorting sounds. But researchers have now shown that some

---

[9]We are so confident of this assertion that we issue a standing challenge. If you can find one impotent animal, we will send you a free copy of this book. Send us two impotent animals, and we will send you two books. Get the idea? Simply mail the animals in a box—with holes so they can breathe—to the American Medical Association offices in Chicago, Illinois. Offer void where hamsters prohibited.

women really are allergic to proteins in the semen of their lovers. Exposure can trigger a massive allergic reaction, as if one were experiencing the world's largest bee sting. With appropriate medical care, almost all victims survive, though they tend to be a little gun-shy after that.

If you suspect that you may be allergic to someone's semen, multiple allergy shots will not help. We recommend keeping a loaded syringe of epinephrine under your pillow. This drug has many actions, including making the heart work much harder, but it will reverse most severe allergic reactions. Be careful not to inject your lover, or the earth may stop moving for him, for good.

In preparation for sex, carefully arrange by your bedside a snakebite kit, a bee-sting kit, a hayfever mask, a medicated inhaler, and a pollen counter. You never know what else might be going around.

After considering these dysfunctions and their implications, we cannot help feeling that the human race has somehow lost its way. The rest of the animal world has an approach to disease that is mature, simple, almost casual. Admittedly, extremist tendencies exist among some species, such as an inclination to devour one's spouse if one is not concentrating. But these aberrations are more than compensated for by nature's decision to relegate sex to a few annual days of hysteria, with the rest of the year devoted to eating bark, making strange noises, and so forth.

Do animals discuss senile impotence or hot-tub climaxes with Phil Donahue? Do animals wear underpants that say, "I Can't Help It, I'm Italian"? Do animals go out and buy extracts of sweat glands from dead rodents so they can get live ones to pay for dinner and a drink at my place afterward? Do animals read (or write) articles like "The Gnu You: A 53-Year Make-Over Plan to Give More Style to Your Bounce and Make You More Attractive to the Pepsi Generation"?

No.

Human beings were not always so confused; but then they weren't always human beings.[10] We still share fundamental desires with our evolutionary predecessors for food, drink, loose shoes, and a good neighborhood. But millennia ago, humans began walking upright in high heels, and removing bottle caps with their teeth to impress prospective mates. Eventually, carnal knowledge alienated us from the rest of the natural world, and the chances that the natural world will take us back diminish with each passing day.

If only we could swallow our mortal pride, and learn from our lower friends, such as the lobster. Technically, these crustaceans are considered members of the cockroach family.[11] But among animals, lobsters have always enjoyed a reputation for a sexual life characterized by sincerity and a sense of mutual sharing. Indeed, the closer one studies lobsters, the more relevant they become to "the human case."

Like professional baseball players, lobsters reach sexual maturity at 6 to 7 years of age. Unlike most athletes, however, lobsters are still active well after the age of 40. They live in small caves, in densely packed communities. The male lobster is bigger than the female lobster, and is the homemaker; he picks a cave whose size is proportional to his own, and becomes its only permanent inhabitant. The females go around the caves in groups. They do the choosing; they like big caves. After a female finds the male she prefers, she moves into the cave.

The male and female lobster then sit face to face and pump seawater at each other. When the male can no longer endure the excitement, he stands up and rubs the female with his antennae. She sheds her hard shell and, as an erotic counterbalance, becomes progressively limp. When she is unable to walk, mating occurs.

How pathetic customs like wet-T-shirt contests seem beside this majestic ritual! Of course, it is easier to describe such virtues in others

---

[10]Although anthropologists have now shown that even two million years ago, there were complaints about morning breath.

[11]Which explains why some Louisiana restaurants list cockroaches (*blatte*) in the seafood section.

than perfect them in ourselves. Still, we urge our patients to adopt an attitude that is less neurotic and more natural. We say that sex for them should be no different than sex is for other animals: Spontaneous! Joyful! Guiltless! Just don't catch any diseases. Also, no smoking afterward.

The road to healthy sexuality is pretty simple then, isn't it? All you need is the human equivalent of the lobster's cave—a place where you never walk, where dozens of people come to your bed every day, undress you, rub your back, and ply you with drugs that alter your senses. If you watch television, you know that there are only two such places—Club Med and any community hospital.

Unfortunately, you cannot just walk into a hospital and expect sexual fulfillment, unless you are already on the staff. Hospitals have long recognized that they are sought by hypochondriacs with the same kind of admiring fascination that Susan George evoked in *Straw Dogs*. They have accordingly designed their version of an electric bug-zapper: the emergency room, designed to attract and then neutralize the worried well. Getting past the emergency room and into the hospital without being sick is going to require an awfully good story. You will find one in the next chapter.

How to Get
Into the Hospital

Getting into the hospital does not carry the prestige of, say, getting into Yale. Indeed, to the casual observer, there are drawbacks to hospitals that make even four years in New Haven seem reasonable. For example, room and board in a hospital make college tuition fees seem like chicken feed. More importantly, contacts made in the hospital rarely prove useful for future gain. At a hospital, the old-boy network works primarily at just getting older, and usually can't remember its shoe size, much less the name of the bright young man whose seminar the previous day ("Pain: Solipsistic or Just Stupid?") was so impressive.

Still, the discerning patient understands quite well why getting into the hospital can be so much harder than getting into college, especially if you don't have the connections. Hospitals, after all, do so much more for the soul than the private school of your choice. For example, few colleges will send a clergyman to your room; in hospitals, they come without your asking. If you want drugs at Stanford, you have to go to the library; in hospitals, nubile young women bring them to you as you lie in bed. At Yale, you have to go to the bathroom; in hospitals, your bathroom comes to you.

Not surprisingly, we all feel a nameless attraction to hospitals and their emergency rooms. We go to the hospital because it is there, because the lights are on and someone must be up, because the doctor's office is closed and it's too early to go to the all-night drug-store and see what's new in laxatives. With shocking regularity, though, the would-be patient is turned away at the door, his complaint deemed too trivial for admission—an experience every bit as humiliating as getting those thin envelopes in April. Thus you learn that you can't check into a hospital for a tune-up at your convenience. All too often the way is barred by penny-pinching insurance companies, hostile triage nurses, and sleepy interns ready to tell you to take your anxiety attack and blow it out your ear.

It doesn't seem fair. You pay your taxes. You don't litter much. You'd hire the handicapped if a really attractive one came along, say like Jon Voight in *Coming Home* or Audrey Hepburn in *Wait Until Dark*. Why shouldn't you have all the medical tests you want when you want them? "We put a man on the moon, Dr. Schreiner," you moan. "Why can't we put me in the hospital?"

Well, we can. We have developed an approach that has been highly successful in gaining admission for even the most timid of patients. (Several of our patients have competed at the national level at the National Institutes of Health in Bethesda, Maryland.) Unlike alternative plans, ours does not demand being double-jointed, wearing expensive Medicalert bracelets, or having the ability to hold your breath and lie really still. If you can remember the phrase "Melvin Belli," you have the talent to get admitted to any hospital any time, sleep all day, eat custard out of little tins, and take drugs even the Pope can't get simply by asking for them.

The first principle of our plan is to resist the temptation to go to academic teaching hospitals in order to make your admission more prestigious. This error makes the admissions process much more complicated. Doctors there are very susceptible to hints of rare diseases, which can seem an advantage. Mention a family history of Grahmann's syndrome—which involves mysterious fevers with periodic psychotic episodes, obesity, and underdeveloped gonads—and watch the entire staff mobilize. The tests ordered after admission are especially comprehensive if the disease to be excluded is extraordinarily exotic. They will cause many curious sensations and may make you glow in the dark.

Unfortunately, such patients run the constant risk of detection, upon which they will be severely punished. At many academic institutions, for example, exposed malingerers have to eat their hospital dinner twice. At Harvard Medical School, they are forced to see a different medical student each day, sometimes two—a brutal but entirely legal form of interrogation that has been known to empty entire wards.

So, when you are just looking to get away from it all, we recommend choosing a nonacademic community hospital. Some of our patients have passed on helpful hints on how to pick them out. Look for a hospital situated on a lonely stretch of highway near an old house high on a windswept hill. If the hospital sign is in blinking neon, with a Coca-Cola or Budweiser logo, you're on the right track. The nurse may collect your wallet, rings, and car keys before the doctor has seen you. This development means you are about to be admitted or about to be robbed—maybe both.[1] If the doctor requires an interpreter to ask you about your insurance coverage, you've found your new home.

In the emergency room, you should complain of a common ailment that cannot be quickly diagnosed and that requires admission to avoid legal complications. Thus we are going to tell you about three symptoms that *cannot be ruled out in the emergency room.* Each requires hospitalization for observation. Each differs as to the tests and drugs

---

[1] If they take your belt and shoelaces, however, think seriously about leaving. And don't do your bird imitations to relieve the tedium of sitting in the waiting room. You're only asking for trouble.

you will get. Your choice will depend on the mood you are in, your religious whims, and whether you've been thrown out of that hospital before. For example, if you are neurotic about having sharp objects stuck in your back, number three (meningitis) may not be for you. That's why we'll begin with the Model T of chief complaints, the people's choice—chest pain.

Chest Pain

For millions of Americans each year, "chest pain" is the magic phrase that opens the doors and parts the red tape. Not surprisingly, it is also the password for sophisticated patients everywhere. They know that many of the tests for myocardial infarctions do not turn positive for hours or even days, and that some heart attacks never show up on tests at all.

They also know that most doctors have heard of cases in which a patient, usually a friend of the powerful, came to the emergency room complaining of a vague discomfort. The patient was reassured that it was indigestion and sent out, only to die several hours later while trying to fill his prescription for Rolaids. Such cases are called "instructive" by physicians—they teach us to write illegibly. In contrast, within the legal profession these tragedies are known as "home-run balls."

So if you come to the emergency room complaining of chest pain, the doctors will try to determine if it is related to the heart. If there's any doubt, you will be admitted to a nice quiet intensive-care-unit bed, where you will get mood-altering drugs and be allowed to rest. If you play your cards right, you can be there a week.

First and foremost, you need the right story. You must tell the first person you see that you are having chest pain. Many of our patients add the adjective "crushing," but others avoid it as a cliché. In any case, those words will immediately get you wheeled into a special room, while other patients, who have lesser problems like pneumonia and knife wounds, look on jealously from the waiting area.

In will come the intern or resident. He is apt to be irritated and a bit skeptical after a night of treating students who have consumed a bottle of One-a-Day Vitamins in a suicide gesture. He'll be ready to flatten any hysteric who wanders into his cage, so your next few words and actions are crucial. You must look anxious, as heart attacks typically cause a sense of terror that is out of all proportion to the pain. Repeatedly mutter that you think you're going to die. Remind the doctor that a fundamental rule of medicine is never to ignore a tip from the jockey. Breaking into a cold sweat is a nice touch.

The intern will usually sneer and ask you if the pain is sharp, or burning, or worse when you take a deep breath. These questions are all ploys to write your pain off as coming from the lungs or stomach—anywhere but the heart. Breathing rapidly and rolling your eyes, you must reply that the pain isn't sharp, that it's more like a pressure in the middle of your chest. Now is the time to play your trump card.

Your knitted brow should suddenly clear in an expression of enlightenment. Make a fist, clutch it to your breast, and wail, *"It feels like an elephant is standing on my chest!"* [2]

Passing out briefly at this juncture will often help drive the point home.

By now you will have the intern's complete attention. He will know that he has a serious problem on his hands. To make conversation while he dries his palms, he may ask you how you feel. Tell him you feel sick to your stomach—rarely a good sign in medicine. Don't mention that what is nauseating you is the fear of explaining yourself to the fire department after insisting on an ambulance ride and then being booted out of the emergency room as a turkey.

The intern will then ask you about cardiac risk factors—the conditions that have been found to increase the likelihood that a patient has heart disease. The strongest of these are:

1. Obesity
2. Diabetes
3. High blood pressure
4. A family history of heart disease
5. Smoking

Obesity is hard to fake. So is diabetes, though it won't hurt to say that you don't think you have it, but your parents, your four grandparents, each of your siblings, and the family St. Bernard all did, and you've never been checked.

At this point, ask if it is okay to light a cigarette with all the oxygen around. Explain that you smoke five to six packs on good days, fewer than that when the coughing gets so bad you can't hold a cigarette

---

[2]This complex is known as the Levine Sign, after the famous Harvard cardiologist Samuel Levine. It is considered unreliable in Africa and India, where trauma victims will sometimes say, "It feels like I'm having a heart attack"—Hannibal's sign.

between your lips, and taking a deep breath causes more blood to appear in your phlegm. The intern may say no.

Continue with your story anyway. Tell him that you aren't positive about the diabetes, because you never knew your family all that well. You never had the chance. After all, you explain, both of your parents died of heart attacks in their early thirties, and none of your brothers or sisters survived to graduate from their high school, St. Jude's Academy for Cardiac Cripples.

You might mention that you were kicked off the St. Jude's chess team for hypertension, but that you never had it treated. Why not? Well, the only trouble it ever gave you was an occasional nosebleed and spells of blurred vision.

By now the intern will be getting a little nervous and may want to examine you. He will check your electrocardiogram (an electrical tracing of your heartbeat that can tell doctors how your heart is working and your most secret thoughts) and take your blood pressure. Thrashing around perhaps faking a convulsion will effectively keep him from finding out that both are normal. He will listen with his stethoscope to your chest, searching for the murmurs, thumps, and whimpers that the heart makes when it is scared, and there is nowhere to run, nowhere to hide. Quietly humming every third note of the theme from *Rocky* may simulate these noises, if he hasn't seen the movie.

In all likelihood, your exam and electrocardiogram are going to be normal. Here the delicate links of trust that you've worked so hard to create will snap like pretzels if you don't take the initiative. Tell him that the pain is starting to shoot into your jaw and left arm. This news will make him review the electrocardiogram and perhaps go for help.

He will return with his resident, and together they may try the Levine Test. This little maneuver involves rubbing a spot on your neck over the carotid artery while asking whether the pain is getting worse. A neurological reflex will make your heart slow down, and if you are having true heart pain, the ache may diminish.

Those who are not having heart pain but desperately want to please their doctor will say that, yes, the pain *is* getting worse. The resident will respond by ripping off the sheets and showing the sheepish patient the door. To avoid an ugly confrontation, we recommend pausing and saying in a puzzled voice, "Why, this may sound crazy, but I think the pain is actually getting better . . . "

If the resident tries to repeat the Levine Test by wrapping both hands around your windpipe and squeezing, he may be on to you.

Usually, though, the doctors will know that they are beaten. The intern will prepare for your admission to the coronary care unit. He may ask you whether you are still having chest pain. Nod yes vigorously (not too vigorously). Then you will experience the happy surprise of morphine percolating from your veins to the frontal lobes of your brain.

The doctors will check every few minutes to see if your pain has abated. As long as you can muster a grimace, the morphine will flow. The opiates will induce a sense of well-being and bonhomie, not to mention the sudden conviction that with one deft shortcut, you have attained the ecstatic center of the spiritual universe. Your ability to convey sincere pain, finely honed after a lifetime of mental self-abuse, may be blunted. More likely, though, you will do as your father did during your conception and drift off into a happy sleep, unclouded by thoughts of tomorrow's consequences.

Appendicitis

Many patients suffer from the delusion that having appendicitis is the work of children. Doctors, though, know that children are busy enough with chicken pox, school, and learning how to smoke. Most children simply do not have time to have their appendix out; they survive into adulthood with these time bombs intact and ticking.

What is appendicitis? To answer this question, one must first ask what is the appendix, and, as far as we can tell, no one really knows. The best medicine can do is describe it as a wormlike pocket that hangs off the end of the large bowel, much as Florida relates to the East Coast. It's usually just a matter of time until it gets plugged up and inflamed, and then performs its only known function—paying for some surgeon's season tickets.

To simplify matters, we tell our patients with appendicitis, "Part of your body has turned on you and is attacking you from within." They are rarely surprised, and this perspective helps prepare them for surgery.

As a way of getting into the hospital, appendicitis has its drawbacks. Chief among them are that a virtuoso performance is rewarded with a knife in the side. Beyond that, there's little chance for an encore, no matter how thoroughly the symptoms are mastered. Finally, you don't get any morphine until after the operation.

But behind every cloud is a chrome hospital bed, and patients who have had their chest pain debunked should not be afraid to come back with an ache below the belt. Giving a good story is easy. The manifestations of appendicitis are so varied that surgeons will listen to almost any complaint—pain, hiccups, horrid age spots—and say, "That's consistent with appendicitis. Get the operating room ready." Once the operation is under way and a normal appendix has been found, the surgeon will be forced to vouch for your story out of embarrassment— more than one doctor has prepared an appendix for the pathology lab by dropping the specimen on the floor and stepping on it. When all is said and done, you'll be left with a nice scar to show on dates.

The key, then, is selling the surgeon. Though we have pointed out that he will often accept a pretty lame story, it's courteous to provide a classic presentation. Tell him the problem began as an ache around the navel, but then the pain became much sharper and moved down and to the right. Many patients say the pain gives them an urge to move their bowels, or pass wind, but it would probably be a bad idea to do either while the surgeon is there. You'll want him rested for surgery.

He will base his decision of whether to operate on both the physical examination and the status of his tax audit. During the exam he will be looking for evidence that the lining of the abdominal wall has become inflamed. Patients with appendicitis keep their abdomens as rigid as boards and demonstrate what doctors call "rebound tenderness"—that is, when the doctor presses down with his hands and then abruptly takes them away, the patient jumps in pain. (It's even more fun than it sounds.) Extra points are awarded if the patient dislodges a ceiling tile.

If rebound is present, most surgeons will take you to the operating room. Their motto, after all, is: *"Ubi dubitas, ex flagellatum."* (When in doubt, whip it out.) On the other hand, if your surgeon checks for rebound by bouncing you off the floor, you may want to try another hospital.

The surgery is brief, and complications are rare. In a couple of days you'll be sitting up, plucking at that string on your hospital gown, calling for more painkillers. And while recovering, do not despair that you only had one appendix and now it is gone, never to get you into a hospital again. Look at matters philosophically, and remember that that is why God gave us the gall bladder.

Viral Meningitis

Our third syndrome offers an attractive alternative to having someone with hairy arms muck around inside your abdomen. It also beats trying to sleep in a coronary care unit amid the background roar of beeping machines and cardiac arrests. Finally, since it is contagious, this ailment will also discourage your doctors from bothering you more than once a day.

This disease, of course, is viral meningitis. It is an illness caused by a viral infection of the meninges, the covering of the brain. While you are ill, the key symptom is severe headache, much worse than the sort used for emergency birth control. Like birth control, however, it is associated with a mild degree of drowsiness and confusion. If these states are not dramatically different from your baseline way of life, you may want to add sore throat, nausea, neck stiffness, and convulsions.

Viral meningitis clears over several days without treatment other than painkillers; full recovery is the rule. The danger lies not in this disease, but in its similarity to the early stages of other, more serious infections that can inflame the brain and eventually cool the cortex. Meningitis caused by bacteria, for example, can leave your brain permanently on the rinse cycle if not treated promptly. Either syphilis or tuberculosis can cause similar symptoms. (People who cough at the wrong moment have been known to end up with both at the same time.) Thus doctors are often obliged to admit patients with viral meningitis for observation until these less pleasant illnesses are ruled out.

So come in complaining of a stiff neck, severe headache, and sore throat. Wear a pair of underpants on your head, talk wildly of Lady Bird Reagan, and throw up on the intern's shoe. Have a convulsion. (Remember that real convulsions are followed by several minutes of profound weakness and confusion. Bouncing right up and asking, "How was that?" is not going to help your case.)

Chances are you will be admitted for several days of observation and a few simple tests. For example, they may take an X ray of your head, which, when framed, makes an inexpensive personal Christmas gift for your parents. More ominously, though, you will have to undergo a spinal tap. A spinal tap is a procedure that involves inserting a needle through your back into the base of the spine in order to sample the fluid that bathes the brain and spinal cord. It's like drilling for oil, except that hitting a pocket of natural gas is not so much a cause for celebration as a reminder to check that one's malpractice insurance premiums are paid up.

The spinal tap is performed with you sitting or lying on your side with your back exposed to the intern, who is holding the needle, and to the resident, who is holding the intern. During the course of the tap, you will probably hear the six most commonly used lies in medicine:

1. I've done this a million times.
2. This won't hurt a bit.
3. Here's a little bee sting.
4. The worst is over now.
5. We're almost done.
6. Now that wasn't so bad, was it?

If a medical student is also present, you may overhear a number of technical comments during the procedure, including:

1. Thanks for letting me try it. This is great. I feel like a real doctor.
2. Does spinal fluid usually smell this bad?
3. Where is all the blood coming from?
4. Have you ever seen anything like this before?
5. I can't get it out. Should we call the surgeons?
6. Wow!

All this brings up a rather painful issue. Sometimes the challenge of getting into the hospital is exceeded only by the challenge of surviving what happens once you're there. After a while, searching tests and powerful drugs can lose their charm. So it's likely that after several days of breakfast and bathroom in bed, when the heart attack has been ruled out, the appendix whipped out, and the spinal fluid drained out, you will be ready to make a bid for freedom. And, in fact, matters usually resolve themselves satisfactorily; patients leave feeling refreshed and ready to take on their medicine cabinets.

But not always. Unfortunately, it is remarkably easy to get sick in the hospital, particularly if you have been under the supervision of a doctor rather than, say, an orderly. Medicine, after all, is not an exact science, but an art. Each test, each treatment represents a calculated risk. Every doctor who is honest with himself knows that he has learned some lessons from mistakes; that's why we call our work "practice."

So if you have been in the hospital for far longer than you expected, if you have been in so long that your hospital number was retired in a moving half-time ceremony, it may be time for you to make the first move. Cancel your Medicaid or Blue Cross, and tell the hospital administrators that you have lost all your money by investing in Italian-Ethiopian war bonds. You will be shipped home by overnight mail.

You can start all over again in the morning.

Tissues
and Answers

Over the years, many patients have written to us in the misguided assumption that we write a popular health advice column. Faithfully answering these letters in order to alleviate needless suffering has been an incredible nuisance. To forestall the expected avalanche of whining missives that will be the public's response to this book, we are publishing a list of the most common questions we hear and our medically informed, compassionate answers.

Q: Over the past week, I have developed a runny nose, a slight temperature, and a cough that doesn't bring up much phlegm. My elderly father also has this same illness. Could it be cancer?
—N.N., Anchorage, Alaska

A: Could be.

Q: I am a chicken trainer, and two days ago I was scratched by one of my chickens while teaching it how to swim. Every time I pick at the scab, it bleeds a little. Should I be worried that it hasn't healed yet?

—Ima Hick, Tyler, Texas

A: Yes.

Q: *When I urinate after a heavy meal, I frequently notice foam in the toilet bowl. Is this cancer?*

—P.R., Media, Pennsylvania

A: Maybe.

Q: *Can you settle a bet? My brother says that Japanese food carries tapeworms, and I say it is the cleanest food in the world. Who's right? The loser has to disembowel himself.*

—E.H., Osaka, Japan

A: So sorry, your brother is correct. Raw fish, a favorite in your country, is often infested with a tapeworm called *Diphyllobothrium latum* (pronounced like the Los Angeles suburb). This parasite's eggs are carried by fish who swim where raw sewage is dumped and make the mistake of not holding their breath. Once a fish is cooked, the tapeworm eggs are no longer dangerous. However, cooks who sample lutefish or gefilte as they are preparing them often become infected. In these and other patients, the tapeworms can live up to twenty years, and grow to a length of twenty feet while causing problems like low blood counts, fatigue, and the blues.

The best way to avoid tapeworms is to avoid fish from contaminated waters, and to cook all freshwater fish thoroughly. There is no fool-proof way to determine which fish in the market are egg carriers, though several of our strangest patients have described methods of fish selection that have worked for them. We pass them on to you:

1.   At the supermarket, pick up the prospective fish purchase and shake it vigorously near your ear. If you

hear anything loose, put the fish down at once. Stick your fingers into nondairy creamer to kill any eggs that might have come off on your hands. If the supermarket security people start giving you a hard time while you are testing all the fish in the market, tell them that your mind is being controlled by Barry Manilow, and let your eyes mist over. They will leave you alone.

2. Place the prospective fish purchase to one side and stare straight ahead. If you see the fish making a movement out of the corner of your eye, and it suddenly stops when you stare at it, there are tapeworms inside. Set the package on fire immediately.

3. If you are unable to test the fish in the market, bring it home and place it on the kitchen table with a tape recorder next to it. While you are making a coughing noise, turn the recorder on. Casually mention to no one in particular that you are going upstairs for a nap. Come back in fifteen minutes, take the recorder up to your room, and replay the tape. If you hear the tiny sounds of a bon voyage party, with clinking glasses and shouted worm toasts, those little bastards are in there.

Q: *Catherine the Great. Did she die the way I think she did?*
—J. Breeling, Chicago, Illinois

A: No, that was Nelson Rockefeller.

Q: *My little daughter gets hiccups all the time. It's hurting her grades in school and driving us crazy at home. We're desperate. Can you help us?*

—Y. Knott, Omaha, Nebraska

A: Your daughter should be seen by a physician to rule out the presence of any disease that can cause hiccups (see "Common Complaints"). Probably none will be found, and your daughter will turn out to have either benign idiopathic hiccups that may pass with time, or else just plain bad manners. In either case, we recommend holding a pillow over her face for fifteen minutes. She won't have hiccups anymore, plus her shoe size will never change again.

Q: I've heard a lot of stories, and I'm hoping you can set me straight. Will, you know, touching yourself make you blind or drive you crazy?

—O. Nan, San Francisco, California

A: It's too soon to tell.

Q: Because my medical problems are so rare no doctor can diagnose them, I've had to see 128 different physicians in the last year. Some of them try to rush me out of the office after only an hour or so, but I've found that faking a language barrier or congenital deafness can stretch most encounters into the better part of an afternoon.

Seeing lots of doctors for one visit each was fun while I was young, and it's a great way to stockpile Valium prescriptions for three-day weekends. But it's boring. I think it must be psychologically destructive for me to have to start from scratch every time. I'm ready to settle down now with just one physician, and I want your help. How can I find Dr. Right?

—R.L., Queens, New York

A: Your concern is completely appropriate. Choosing the right doctor is even more important than disinfecting the bathroom. He's the one who is going to have to sign all those insurance forms. Without his cooperation, your obsessions could get very expensive. Thus he will be a central figure in your life. In selecting yours, you should look for the right combination of credentials, credulity, and credit ratings. Some clues:

Take a look around when you are ushered into his office to await his arrival. Are there bars over the window? Is there a bar on the first floor? Are the free drug samples easily accessible so you can put them in your pocket without having to ask every time? Look for pictures of his children on his desk. Do they resemble game fish? Is there a picture of a wife in a family setting, or has someone placed a piece of black electrical tape over her face?

Is the language on his diploma in an alphabet you recognize? The further it is from Indo-European roots, the better off you are. Does his name end in a vowel or a grunt? Is his first name only two letters? Do the certificates on his wall include a high school award for good citizenship? Is it signed by a dictator?

When he comes in, check him out. Do his socks match? Do his eyes match? Is there evidence of superficial skin ulcerations? Does he breathe with his mouth open? Would you describe the color of the earpieces on his stethoscope as "earth tones"?

Tell him there is an official from the Drug Enforcement Agency waiting to talk with him in the lobby. See if he leaves by the door or window. Examine his desk. See how many investment counselors and attorneys are listed in his Rolodex. See if there are any listings under "parole officer." Are there prescription pads engraved with several different names? Does his medical license come with interchangeable photos? Look in his white coat for toys.

With these tips, you should be able to find a doctor who is right for you, plus enough dirt to keep him in line for years to come. These years will be filled by return visit after return visit. Yours will be a relationship richer than most marriages, full of themes, and beneath them, counterthemes. Underneath these, there will be countercounter-themes. And underneath *those,* there will be free parking. Every visit will be anticipated for days in advance and mulled over for days after-ward. By then it will be time to start anticipating your next appoint-ment, the next confrontation between two old and familiar rivals. Ali and Frazier. The Celtics and the 76ers. Dog and cat. You and your doctor.

Good luck to you, and remember that today is the last day of your life so far.

Q: Is it true that the government is trying to give us cancer by putting poison in the IRS forms that you inhale when filling them out?
—G.S., New Haven, Connecticut

A: Could be.

Q: *Are old people really interested in sex?*
                                   —*K.C., Pittsburgh, Pennsylvania*

A: Yes, they are. The only problem is that they sometimes mis-
place it.

Q: *I am worried about becoming infested with parasites. I am
God-fearing; I don't smoke or eat. I don't watch* Those Incredible
Animals. *I do not kiss anyone who is not American. What is a parasite
anyway, and how do you catch them?*
                                   —*G.B., Wellesley, Massachusetts*

A: Parasites are dirty crawling things that are uglier than Milton
Berle in a dress. They are the principal export of Chad and are considered a delicacy in Libya, but nowhere else.

They are everywhere. They are found in dirt, under fingernails, over
Baltimore, on walls, on barbers' combs, and in lawyers' briefs. Some
parasites burrow into your skin, while others like to be inhaled. A few
drift gently into your eyes as you sleep, while many are night deposits
dropped into your bloodstream by ambitious mosquitoes. There are
parasites that live in your intestines, whose eggs can clog your liver
like lemons in a toilet. There are parasites that work in your blood
cells and play in your brain.

Take *Naeglaria.* Please. This baby is a germ that lives in lakes and
swims up your nose and into your brain. With *Naeglaria,* you don't get
egg roll, you become one. Another reason not to fall when waterskiing.

These self-sufficient cells can do anything you can do better, especially multiply. They're pretty good at subtracting, too, if you catch our
drift. No one knows why they prefer renting over home ownership, or
even why they exist. Recent findings suggest that they were put on this
earth by a vengeful God.

Q: *I'm a 23-year-old blonde, and my friends tell me that I'm attractive. That doesn't have anything to do with what I'm writing about,*

but I bet it caught your attention. I love diet soda, and, in fact, drink about twenty cans a day of a lo-cal brand that comes from an offshore oil well near New Jersey. It's that lemon-lime drink they advertise on television as the only soda that glows in the dark. I have to drink it fast, because otherwise it tends to eat through the sides of the can.

I say that if I can buy it in a store, then it must be safe. My boyfriend, who recently took out an insurance policy on me, thinks the stuff is dangerous, and that I will end up as a silhouette on Sixty Minutes *making grunting noises while Mike Wallace asks me if I am bitter over the loss of my ears. What do you think?*

—*S.G., Cleveland, Ohio*

A: Our position has always been that almost anything in moderation is safe, and almost anything in excess is dangerous. Cut back to sixteen or seventeen cans a day, and keep checking your ears to make sure that they aren't getting loose.

Q: I have been quite ill with Rocky Mountain spotted fever, which I caught while hunting endangered species near Aspen. I am recovered now, but I don't even remember having been an a mountain with spots. How could I have caught the disease?

—*J.W., Denver, Colorado*

A: You appear to have suffered a certain degree of brain damage as a result of your infection. The high temperatures can occasionally cause premature thawing of your cerebral fishsticks. We appreciate the amount of effort it must have taken to write us. As a gift, we are sending you a subscription to *US.* Stay home, mix yourself a glass of water, and read it. Don't write us again.

Q: Is Slim Whitman a diet candy?

—*J.W., Denver, Colorado*

A: We told you not to write us again.

Q: Will touching frogs give me warts?

—*G.S., Hicksville, New York*

A: No, that comes from lustful thoughts.

Q: I am writing from a very nice medical center, where I have been hospitalized for three months with recurring bouts of chest pain that the doctors can't seem to figure out. I am an old man with no family, and I like it here. The nurses think I am cute, and I get to wear my cowboy boots in bed. It's fun to walk along with the back of my hospital gown open and not get arrested. Every morning I get my favorite breakfast of eggs and morphine. I am worried that they are going to make me leave if they can't find something wrong. Do you have any suggestions?

—K.T., Chicago, Illinois

A: There is no single thing one can do to prevent getting ejected once the doctors think that there is nothing wrong with you. The most effective strategy for you is to slow the process of evaluation by stalling on every test or procedure that comes up. With luck, a routine admission can be stretched from days to months or even the better part of a decade.

A simple device for prolonging hospitalization is to knock over the receptacle that the nurses are using to collect the twenty-four-hour urine samples the doctor has ordered. They will have to keep repeating it. If they schedule you for an X ray of your stomach because of your constant complaint of abdominal pain, eat something from the other patients' trays just before going down to the radiology department. They will either reschedule you, if you get caught, or diagnose a stomach growth that resembles a lemon Danish. The tests that ensue will be exciting.

If these tactics fail, some of our patients recommend switching beds and identification bracelets with other patients—the MX Plan. Another strategy is to write notes in your own chart, pretending that you are a consultant, perhaps the chief of medicine. In your notes, express anger that certain tests have not been done and request that all those completed be repeated. If nothing else works, you can always try dressing up like an intern (unshaven, mismatched socks, stained tie, gummy stethoscope, 173 pens). They will never let you leave.

Q: I am only four feet tall, I stoop, my spine is covered with ulcerated lumps. My fingernails and toenails are chronically infected; they are thick, scaly, and smell like dead dogs. My complexion is beige, with disfiguring blotches in harvest gold and avocado green. I can't bend any of the joints in my one leg. My drool has resulted in an unsightly fissure on my chin.
Why did God give me a body like this?

—S.K., Los Angeles, California

A: Why do fools fall in love?

Q: I am 105 years old. I have been in the hospital almost eight years this January. I came in to visit my sister and somehow got in the wrong line. They took all my belongings and gave me a pillow-case to wear. My bed has a view of a curtain, but a nice curtain. I have a large airy room, which I share with twenty-five other girls. It's not too bad here. I like the food, and I like my baths, and the noises at night remind me of my camping days when I was a Brownie.
What worries me is this: I don't know what's wrong with me, but I know it must be bad, because every morning for the last five years, the nurses have greeted me by saying, "Oh, what a pleasant surprise!" If I really am dying, I'd like to know it, because I'd like to discuss whether I want heroic measures like a respirator or PAP smear. Unfortunately, I haven't seen a doctor here since 1979. How can I tell whether I am slipping away, and what the doctors intend to do about it?

—R.I.P., Binghamton, New York

A: The question of whether to employ heroic measures for a terminally ill patient is a matter of gravest importance and should be discussed between the doctor and patient to ensure that the patient's wishes are respected. Sometimes, though, the doctor just forgets. It's tough enough just trying to keep up with changes in the tax laws.

Still, there are certain clues as to whether your doctor expects a Christmas card from you next year, clues that might help you decide about planting your garden with annuals or perennials. For example, getting a rosary with your English muffin at breakfast can be a bad sign, as is the nurses' request for you to turn in your oxygen mask when you are finished. If your doctor leaves a brochure of group tours to Lourdes, you have a legitimate cause for concern. It's also worrisome if they move your bed over by the elevator, or if you find the nurses using your chest X rays as placemats.

One final piece of advice to guide investment strategy—if more than ten percent of your body now rests in various biopsy jars, it would be best to stick with term insurance.

TERMINAL MUFFIN

Examination of the Self

The Examination of the Self is such a natural and essential part of our day, we often forget that you don't know how to do it. But we certainly understand your desire to learn. As this book has already shown, the danger from within is always present, and your body is less a vessel than an anonymous threat. Since most doctors examine patients only once a year, by the time an illness is detected, it has often reached the stage we call "Too Late." Thus, it's up to you to fill the void between annual physicals with punishing self-scrutiny—the only thing that stands between you and immortality without fainting.

This reliance on the Examination of the Self fits in perfectly with the new militancy popular among patients today. People have assumed responsibility for their own health, though with more than a little ambivalence. The willingness to assume command of what seems a sinking ship follows a bitter realization—that they are prisoners within their own bodies, and that they have incommutable life sentences.[1] To make the best of a bleak situation, they have taken charge of their own bodies. And why not? No one else seems interested.

Unfortunately, this duty often turns out to be more demanding than expected. Examining one's own body requires a sense of vigilance and awareness that adds new levels of meaning to the word "introspection." (It also helps to have several mirrors of flexible handles.) Most of our patients have instinctively devoted their lives to this task. They study their bodies with an attentiveness that is otherwise impossible to duplicate outside the autopsy room. The problem is that they don't know what to do with the data.

To the untrained observer, the body is a well-oiled machine that came without the instructions. Well-intentioned patients try to listen to their bodies with the intensity of musicians listening to a symphony—alert to every change of key and to every broken string, not to mention the gum under the piano bench. But all too often, they just don't understand what they hear.

To our embarrassment, doctors do a pretty shabby job of teaching patients what they need to know—a reflection of the general lack of interest in preventive medicine among physicians in this county. Indeed, many physicians want nothing to do with the patient until something is clearly wrong. Unconsciously, they may even try to drive the "healthy" patient away with subtle gestures—especially if he is a frequent visitor. Some end sessions abruptly by announcing, "See you *next year*. Get it? *Next* year." Others stamp "Do not open before Christmas" on the patient's chart as he looks on, or, better yet, simply toss it in the trash. When these tactics fail the doctor may try passing out during the examination, explaining upon regaining consciousness that he has had this problem for months, that the spells are coming closer and closer together, and that he can't figure out what is wrong for the life of him.

So we wanted this, the crowning chapter of this book, to provide

---

[1]See the best-selling treatise *Our Bodies, Our Cells.*

you with all the instruction you need to develop your own routine for constant monitoring of your vital and not-so-vital bodily functions. With the aid of this information, you should be able to scrutinize each tissue each day for disease—a process we call the Organ Recital. Every morning, before pronouncing all systems go, you will put yourself through a meticulous checking, double-checking, and checking yet again that makes NASA's preparations for a moon shot seem a romp in the woods. With any luck, you'll find something slightly amiss, abort your mission for the day, and head directly back to bed.

Where to begin? It has been said that your face is the mirror of your soul. (It has also been said that your face is uglier than a dead frog in a bowl of punch.) Finding something on it that everyone else already knows about but has been afraid to mention is no fun. Thus we urge our patients to begin their examinations with the head's various orifices—the ears, nose, and throat. If you have any other orifices in your head, we don't want to know about them. We just ate.

Ear, Nose, and Throat

No area of medicine is as baffling for the layman as the ear, nose, and throat—abbreviated as ENT by patients, but called otorhinolaryngology (rhymes with "tremendous fee") by physicians to keep patients off balance and remind them who's boss. One reason is that the anatomy is so complex: interconnecting tubes, spirals, and blind passages abound. If the whole mess wasn't so small and filled with mucus, it would be a great place to play Dungeons & Dragons.

Instead, the ear, nose, and throat serves as a wonderland for children who are discovering their own bodies, and haven't gotten to the good parts yet (see "The Hypochondriac's Guide to Sexual Dysfunction"). Events occur together that seem magically, if somewhat randomly linked. Kids blow their noses, and suddenly they can't hear. They are eating lunch, and someone makes them laugh; incredibly, milk shoots out of their noses. Their ears feel funny on an elevator; they swallow, and all is well. Out of nothing, their bodies fashion

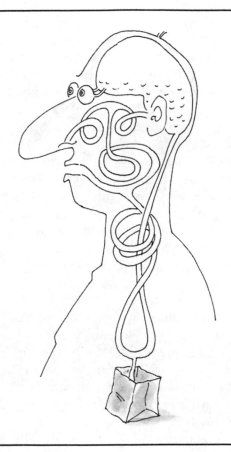

lumps of wax and whatever. They ask their parents to account for these miracles, and they are told to go watch television. Thus they learn for the first time that we do not live in a rational world.

As children grow older, go to school, and mature, they learn to accept the body's idiosyncrasies and inside jokes, and even laugh along, as if they get it, too. They may never figure out how that milk got into their noses, but after a while they stop asking why. There are, in addition, real otorhinolaryngological mysteries to ponder. For example—what is that tiny hunk of flesh hanging down in the back of your throat? (Answer: the uvula. Many adolescents worry about the small size of their uvulas. These unfortunates answer ads in the backs of comic books for creams and exercises guaranteed to increase the size of their uvulas and therefore their popularity. Such gimmicks simply do not work. Accept the remnant that nature gave you, and work on developing other aspects of your personality.)

Given the delicacy and complexity of this area of the body, even routine maintenance is fraught with danger, and doctors do little to defuse the problems. Tasks as simple as cleaning one's ears are made out to be work for neurosurgeons or priests, sometimes both. Doctors will tell you that if you use a Q-Tip, you will jam wax into your brain's parietal lobes, after which your brain will leak fluid until it resembles dried dog food. But ask a physician what *he* uses, and why he has all those Bic pen tops lying around. He will set off his beeper and immediately leave the room.

Not surprisingly, the turf is a virtual breeding ground for bad news. Minor complaints like a runny nose can mean lethal midline granuloma, leprosy, or syphilis, while seemingly subtle variations from the norm may spell disaster. Are your teeth too far apart? You could have a pituitary tumor that is making your jaw grow. Too much saliva? Someone might be poisoning you with arsenic. Too *little* saliva? You may have Sjogren's syndrome, in which your salivary glands race the rest of you across the River Styx.

Understanding the pathophysiology of these diseases is beyond most laymen—*we* gave up after two years of medical school. Instead, we rely on two tried-and-true, all-purpose remedies—antihistamines and hot-and-sour soup. One or a combination of these two is effective in ninety percent of otorhinolaryngological emergencies.

Beyond that, we teach our patients a *functional* self-examination— that is, one that tests the functions of the ear, nose, and throat. Thus we ask them to warm up their tongues and throats by saying, "Red leather, yellow leather" three times quickly—first normally, then while holding a half a cup of flour in their mouths. If the flour comes out of any other orifices, see a specialist immediately.

We examine our own hearing by seeing how far we can hold the telephone receiver from our head and still make out the gist of what the patient is calling about. Testing each ear individually is equally simple. While patients are talking to us in the office, we casually stick a finger first in one ear and then the other, and listen for a difference. On both sides, you should be able to pick up many of the key words of the conversation, while hearing a dull, humming noise that specialists call "The Ocean." (For this test to be accurate, the same finger must be stuck in both ears.)

Similar techniques can be used on the nose to test sense of smell, but at the request of our mothers, we won't go into them.

Your Eyeballs

An incredible number of patients come to us full of superstitions about the so-called relationship between deviant sexual behavior and blindness. We sincerely hope that these stories are not true. Still, a great many other things can happen to your eyes, and almost none of them are good. Worst of all, most of these diseases begin with subtle signs that can be easily missed, especially if you're not seeing so well.

For example, how long has it been since you checked if your eyeballs stick out too far? *Exophthalmos* can mean an overactive thyroid.[2] (Do not worry about this diagnosis if you have no other manifestations of thyroid disease, such as restlessness, occasional palpitations, or insomnia.) Tears may mean infection, arsenic poisoning, or strong emotion, all of which are to be religiously avoided. Other diseases nibble away at the corners of your vision before going in for the big score. Thus we advise our patients to check every few hours on whether they can see things way off to the side.

---

[2]Except in Greece, where it is a popular pet's name.

For obvious reasons, then, you should constantly monitor changes in your visual acuity and in the function of the muscles that move the eyes. There's no need for weekly appointments with the ophthalmologist when you can examine yourself every day by giving your eyes a "stress test."

We like to test our eyes on buses and subways by trying to make out newsprint from three feet away—roughly the distance involved in reading over the shoulder of another passenger. To make sure that we are seeing each word correctly, we read the stories aloud. The paper's owner will usually let you know if you have made a mistake.

Yet another favorite testing technique we apply in hallways and elevators is reading the names on necklaces that women wear. If you need to get closer than six inches, you may be in trouble.

Whenever things get a little slow during a patient visit, we test each eye independently by first closing one eye and then the other. Sometimes this maneuver upsets elderly women, who think that we are winking at them. Such notions evaporate during the next part of our calisthenics, when we test our *medial rectus* muscles—the muscles that turn the eyes inward—by crossing our eyes and producing a double image of two patients. We usually tire of this exercise quickly and move on to the next phase, which is testing the *superior rectus* muscles—the muscles that turn the eyes upward—by pulling on our lower lids and looking up. If you do this correctly, you will look like a Greek statue, and the patient will scream.

Lastly, we test the *lateral rectus* muscles, which turn the eyes to the sides, by turning both eyes outward at the same time. You may feel a sudden temptation to hunt flying insects. This is a primitive reflex that should not be encouraged.

These exercises should ensure that your eye muscles are free of unsightly flab, and prevent that middle-aged bulge that makes most people over 50 look like frogs.

If you have problems with any of these exercises or tests, you should see a reputable optometrist,[3] as you may need corrective lenses. These will make you look smarter and will clink like champagne glasses when you kiss someone else with spectacles. But they do have serious side effects, and you should be prepared for irreversible changes in the way you relate to the opposite sex.

Doctors have found that men who wear glasses spend half of their waking lives trying to avoid situations in which they might get slapped. They know that when they get slapped, they won't look rakish and

[3]A reputable optometrist is one who does not make you remove your clothes for the examination.

even more attractive, like a Bogart or a Gable. Their glasses go flying across the room. They get these ridiculous little cuts on the bridges of their noses. They have to figure out where their glasses landed by the sound and by squinting in the general direction of the woman's follow-through. When they do find their glasses, the frames won't sit straight on their faces anymore. The woman offers to pay to have them fixed. It's humiliating for everyone involved.

Thus few men who wear glasses get slapped more than once in their lives—and usually that's by their mothers, who don't really count. Instead, they develop a style around women reminiscent of the foreign policy of France—they sort of hang around the edges of the fray, hoping something good will fall into their laps.

Some men tire of living in fear of sudden violence followed by myopia. They buy eyeglass straps, of the sort worn by professional baseball players and chemistry majors. Others invest in contact lenses—a psychodynamic switch equal in significance to a sex change. Some even stop wearing corrective lenses altogether. They end up seeing less but enjoying it more.

Obesity

Patients often ask us how they can tell whether they are truly over-weight or just have heavy bones. This question is more difficult than one might think. The Metropolitan Insurance Co. once published a famous set of tables that defined "normal" body weight according to height, but it was so controversial that they could only get it printed on the backs of rulers. The U.S. Air Force developed a different set of standards taking into account age, degree of activity, and how fast you fall without a parachute. Other approaches, equally scientific, involve lean body mass, surface area of the body, and how long the elastic band of your underpants lasts.

These aren't much help to the plump hypochondriac trying to go it alone. At what point, you ask yourself as you gaze into the mirror, should I start worrying about my weight?

Of course, if you are forced to gaze into two mirrors, the answer is pretty clear. But for the rest of you, we have developed a set of practical criteria that do not require special equipment or a medical degree, and can be answered in the privacy of your own home:

1. When you are sitting in a park, do children think you are a ride?

2. Can you hear echoes in your navel?

3. Do you have to travel by wide-body jet?

4. Are you sometimes used to show home movies on?

5. Are you forced to pay state road taxes and to check in at weighing stations while driving on interstate highways?

6. Are you unable to remember the last time anyone would sit on a seesaw with you?

7. When you get on a bus, does it register "Tilt" and refuse to give you your money back?

If your answer to any of the questions above is yes, you are overweight and should start working on an anxiety reaction immediately. If your answer to all of them is yes, then go back to the chapter entitled "Ten Diseases You Were Better Off Not Knowing About" and reread the section on Prader Willi syndrome very carefully.

In any case, we recommend developing a weight-reduction program that includes not only a carefully planned diet but meticulous attention to your weight itself and how it changes throughout the course of the day. For example, weighing yourself before and after meals, especially when dining out, can give you a new perspective on just how much you are chowing down. Of course, most of these weight "gains" are erased in the following hours by perspiring, blowing your nose, and throwing up. Weighing yourself before and after any of these activities can be extremely satisfying. Documenting such subtle shifts is not easy, however, and requires that you weigh yourself in *exactly* the same manner every time. Here is our routine:

1. Lock the door.
2. Disrobe.
3. Perform whatever bodily functions you can think of to make yourself lighter. (Don't make us go into them.)
4. Step on scale.
5. Step off scale.
6. See if scale is "zeroed."
7. It is. Try to figure out how much your glasses weigh.
8. Step on the scale again, this time leaning to the left and back. You are now one and one-half pounds lighter. Smile.
9. Weigh yourself again, leaning to the right and forward.
10. Worry.

Your Teeth

A few words about oral care—in fact, *very* few, because like most physicians, we know almost nothing about dentistry. What we do know is this—only bad things can happen in there, and the worst of these usually take place around and during your regular visit to your dentist.

The physical pain is bad enough, especially when combined with the psychological distress provoked by emotion-laden terms like root canal, periodontal scum, and trench mouth. What really hurts, though, is the shame: the disappointment so clearly etched on your dentist's face after he says, "Open up and show me your stuff"; the accusations, so often unspoken;[4] the implications that you could have done better.

---

[4]Not often enough.

There are two ways of dealing with this uncomfortable situation. One is to come back with a snappy retort, like, "What do you want me to do—kill myself?" Another is to try to limit your guilt feelings by making good oral care a habit. It's really tough to choose, but we recommend the latter course and suggest the following routine after each meal:

1. Brush your teeth.
2. Feel lousy about not using dental floss. Recall how the hygienist humiliated you by saying "yeecchh" while working on you three years ago.
3. Take dental floss out of medicine cabinet. Cut off a piece equal to your height multiplied by your waist

size. This should suffice for your upper teeth.

4. Apply with sawing motion between teeth.

5. Wait for bleeding to stop. If it takes too long, you may have leukemia.

6. Consider giving up. Imagine yourself with dentures.

7. Floss a few more teeth.

8. Decide that dentures won't be so bad.

Your Skin

Few organs beg for self-examination as powerfully as the skin, yet it is often overlooked in the restless search for disease. Why do we ignore this marvelous organ, which comes in so many sizes and colors, seals in freshness, and proffers little hairs everywhere you look? Think where we'd be without our skin—unemployed, for one thing. Who'd hire someone that looked like Nat Turner after confession? As Pat Boone used to say, if you have your skin, that's a start.

Our research suggest that patients ignore the skin because of youthful trauma. Typically, during those delicate formative years when lifelong neuroses are gathering strength for the playoffs, an adolescent brings some subtle blotch to his dermatologist. Anticipating cancer, perhaps a rare type that will be named after him, the youth is instead told that the disfiguration is disgusting and due to lust, and dismissed.

Still innocent, the teenager tries several more times: with a zit that refuses to heal, a hair that grows faster than the others, the mysterious scaling between his toes. Finally, the dermatologist gets exasperated, slaps him around, and refuses to see him again. Such treatment should surprise no one, as dermatologists are the most irritable of specialists. Anyone who flays warts for a living serves a dark and hungry god.

Scarred by this experience, the patient can develop such an aversion to dwelling on his dermis that he can't expound upon his skin condition(s) to his doctor(s). In extreme cases, he will stop picking at his scabs and cease weekly charting of the diameter and color of every mole on his body.

This fear not only denies the patient a profoundly satisfying experience; it also invites disaster. For who knows when some little blemish you'd like to think is a hickey will turn out to be the first sign of Dego's disease.

This rare syndrome, also known as malignant atrophic papulosis,[5] affects the entire body, but it usually holds its first surprise party on the skin. A pimple may appear, and then transform into a pale depressed area with a red border, not unlike West Berlin. The lesions are innocent enough to the eye, but microscopically, a small blood vessel has closed itself off, and the surrounding tissue has died.

These dead areas eventually leave unsightly draining infections. That's the good news. The bad news is that the same process is going on throughout your body, causing strokes, heart attacks, and other mischief. The most common culminating event is a sudden perforation of the intestines—a painful catastrophe, particularly if you are having dinner at the home of your boss.

What is the best way to guard against Dego's disease, those horrid age spots, and other warnings that the end is near? Careful inspection of every square inch of skin after each meal is a start. Some areas may be difficult to visualize directly. Polaroid snapshots of these regions will not only give you a good look, but will also provide you with a permanent record for your health-care files. But, for God's sake, lock the door first, okay?

Your Lungs

The lungs are the largest organs in the body, and with good reason. They are essential to three of your most vital bodily functions—coughing, wheezing, and smoking. The respiratory tract has become even

---

[5]Now you know why we call it Dego's disease.

more important with the growing popularity of low-tar and filter cigarettes, for without superb lung function, meeting your minimum daily requirement (MDR) of nicotine is almost impossible.

Even if you don't smoke or live in Los Angeles, the world is full of hazards for your lungs. Ignoring air pollution for a moment, we are almost all subjected to lung toxins at work every day. Cotton workers, for example, get a disease called byssinosis, characterized by dyspnea (shortness of breath), chest tightness, cough, and wheezing. Typically, these symptoms are worse on the first day after a temporary absence—thus the phrase "Monday dyspnea" is often used to describe this disease. Variations on this theme are well known in other occupations and to school children around the world.

Not even fresh country air turns out to be safe. Physicians have known for years about farmer's lung—a chronic lung disease caused by the body's reaction to airborne material produced by moldy hay. And recently, a new entity was described in the *Annals of Internal Medicine* called Dung Lung—not a Vietnamese diplomat, but a respiratory complication of exposure to you-know-what.

Fortunately, the capacity of the lungs to absorb nicotine, nitrous oxide, and other essential vitamins is roughly paralleled by their ability to handle oxygen. Thus you can monitor your own lung function with a few simple tests that can be performed at home, at work, or on your way to the doctor:

1. Hold your breath for an entire visit to the bathroom in a Chinese restaurant.

2. See if you can blow out all the candles on your child's birthday cake while he tries to think of a wish.

3. On the subway, try to make a woman's earrings sway by blowing on them. Then see how far you can run without stopping.

4. Don't breathe for an entire commercial break of *The Tonight Show.*

If you fail at any of these, we recommend taking up smokeless tobacco immediately.

Your Heart

Most Americans are taught in high school that the heart is a pump. Having studied this organ in detail, we find the notion of comparing the power source of the cardiovascular system to a woman's shoe ludicrous. The hemodynamics, the potential problems, the odor—all these are completely different. If the heart is analogous to anything fashioned from human hands, we'd have to say it is a time bomb.

Just as a bomb has only so many ticks on its timer, we feel the heart has only so many lub-dubs to give before planned obsolescence has its way—2,575,400,000 to be exact. Skipping beats won't help. Thus, the examination of the heart should concentrate on accurate determination of the rate at which the heart is beating, and then slowing it down as much as possible.

You can calculate your own pulse rate by listening to your heart for one minute. If you do not have a stethoscope, build one of your own by cutting up the tubes that carry brake fluid in your car and gluing them to Dixie cups. Or you can just feel your own arteries pulsing at your wrist while watching the clock. If you get a rate of zero, either your watch is fast, or you are dead. If you get a pulse of ninety or more, you heart is probably beating too fast, and you should make it slow down at once.

Most people "will" their hearts to slow by only twenty or thirty beats per minute. For further reductions in heart rate designed to get as much time as possible out of your two and a half billion beats, we recommend the following measures:

1. Avoid coffee, tea, and cola.
2. Avoid psychological stress.
3. Sleep as much as possible, at least sixteen or seventeen hours a day.

4. Never run. Walk as little as possible. Use cars or elevators whenever you can.

5. No sex, unless you are married.

6. Have your thyroid gland removed.

The Rest of the Body

Self examination of the organs that lie below the diaphragm is both unpleasant and dangerous—unpleasant, because the names of most tissues down there recall dishes in Cantonese restaurants that you are afraid to order; dangerous, because touching this general area on purpose can be construed as a felony in twenty-three states, and as a traffic violation in many of the rest.

Thus we recommend testing these organs indirectly by subjecting them to physiological stress. Of course, checking out each organ individually is an impractical waste of time. We have found that all systems can be simultaneously tested each morning by simply starting the day with a hearty Mexican meal, washed down by a couple of bottles of Dos Equis beer.

We won't bore you with the science. Suffice it to say that the peppers will test the integrity of your stomach wall, while the fats will put your pancreas into overdrive. Your liver will be stimulated to mass-produce gallstones, while your spleen will be tied up fighting infection. Your kidneys will be busy with the Dos Equis. Finally, your legs will get a good workout, as the tortilla stuffing is immunologically ejected from your bowels as a foreign body.

You have now completed a comprehensive examination of yourself. Do it again. Depressing, isn't it? Now you know why doctors are so moody.

The next step is also up to you. Make an appointment with your doctor so you can give him all the news. You can draw up an alphabetical list of your symptoms to demonstrate how efficient you are.

Your doctor will certainly see you in a new light (assuming he agrees to see you at all).

To gain his complete confidence in your diagnostic skills, you will have to make some attempt to speak his language. Too often the specialist terminology employed by doctors—words like "angioplasty," "thrombolysis, " and "croak"—go right over the patient's head. In order to save face, the patient leaves the office with no real understanding of what the doctor has diagnosed or recommended. Meanwhile, the doctor is chortling to his partner: "Can you believe that? He didn't know he had Landouzy-Dejerine disease! And he still doesn't!"

If you can learn doctor-talk, you will not only gain your doctor's respect, you'll begin to share his values, his attitudes—maybe even a stock tip or two. You can make a start by mastering the terms in the glossary that follows. Once fluent, you will be qualified to go anywhere and tell anyone anything. Just like a doctor.

Glossary

ABSCESS, n. A collection of fluid, teeming with bacteria, toxins, and other agents hazardous to health; the body's version of Lake Erie.

ACHROMATURIA, n. Colorless or nearly colorless urine. This finding doesn't mean much, but it's something to look forward to on weekends.

ACNE VULGARIS, n. Inflammatory disease of the sebaceous glands and hair follicles of the skin. Once considered to be caused by bacteria, chocolate bars, and other foods, including fishsticks; now understood to be due to impure thoughts and sneaking money from your parents.

ACROMPHALUS, n. Abnormal projection of the navel. Osler won the Nobel Prize in 1896 for demonstrating that if you press your fingers precisely on the acromphalus, you will have many sons and your daughters will care for you in your old age.

ACUTE, adj. Sudden, without warning, as in the onset of Lassa fever or the departure of the physician who recognizes it.

AKINESIA, n. Without kinesia.

ALBINO, n. Pigment of the imagination.

AMAZIA, n. Without mazia; the medical term for the lack of breast development in females, described by Hippocrates as a disease long before it became chic.

ANESTHESIOLOGIST, n. Operating-room physician who postpones your pain until you receive his bill.

ANOPHORIA, n. Tendency of one eye to drift upward; a syndrome that when witnessed makes children throw rocks and gives adults motion sickness; rarely seen in busy, successful executives.

APPENDIX, n. Useless, vestigial, finger-like projection from the colon; the body's idea of a knock-knock joke.

ATAXIA, n. Without a taxi.

AUTOPSY, n. Diagnostic procedure by which the hypochondriac hopes for vindication.

BACTERIA, n. Really, really tiny microorganisms. Doctors talk about them all the time, but, frankly, we're not even sure they exist.

BILE, n. Bitter alkaline secretion of the liver, thought by the ancients to cause irritability and virtually all other murderous instincts, phenomena now understood to be induced by too much nondecaffeinated coffee.

BITTERLING TEST, n. A real pregnancy test employed early in this century in which a Japanese fish resembling a carp was placed in a quart of fresh water with two teaspoons of a woman's urine. If the woman was pregnant, a tubelike structure protruded from the fish's belly, and festivities or fisticuffs commenced, depending on the context. Though replaced by modern blood tests, many of which do not require killing animals, the Bitterling test survives as a delightful and revealing party game that proves a real conversation piece. Party kits with fish and materials for ten tests are available at a special price to buyers of this book.

BODO, n. Germ found in stale urine, one reason why we always recommend getting it fresh.

BORBORYGMI, n. The gurgling, rumbling sounds made by the passage of gas through the intestines. Traditionally a source of social embarrassment, these noises are what the doctor listens for when he places his stethoscope on your stomach. Although this maneuver is most useful as a source of comic relief after the tedium of feeling for the liver, some doctors have attempted to predict the patient's future by interpreting these sounds, a service that is currently available only in a few academic research centers.

BRACHYGNATHIA, n. Abnormal shortness of the underjaw. People with this syndrome all look like Dorothy Kilgallen and are not to be trusted.

BULIMIA, n. Morbidly increased appetite after a meal, sometimes alternating with anorexia. See **PROSTATE.**

CACOGENICS, n. Race degeneration resulting from the reproduction of inferior gene pools. Perhaps the most poignant modern example of this phenomenon is the Chicago Cubs.

CACOSMIA, n. A neurosis centering on imaginary foul odors. This is so common a complaint among our patients that we have been forced to keep a vase of dead laboratory animals in our waiting room to remind these whiners just how bad things could be.

CAFFEINE, n. A stimulant found in coffee, cola, and tea, known to cause anxiety, palpitations, gastrointestinal distress, and insomnia; used by physicians only when real amphetamines are unavailable.

CEREBELLUM, n. Ante post-bellum and post ante-bellum.

CERVIX, n. Anatomical term referring either to the opening of the uterus or to the bones of the neck—an unfortunate ambiguity that has resulted in several famous operating-room errors.

CHEST PAIN, n. The patient's trump card, his definitive demand for attention; analogous to your mother's threat to tell your father, your father's threat to tell your mother, your wife's threat to tell everyone, or Rona Barrett's threat to tell no one at all.

CHOLESTEROL, n. Fatty substance that renders food palatable; found in abundance in almost everything worth eating, plus Big Macs.

Every American has a special place in his heart for this lipid compound— his coronary arteries.

CHRONIC, adj. Describing an entity that will not go away, despite the doctor's best efforts; sometimes a disease, often a patient.

CLITORIS, n. Mythological part of the female genitalia popularized by feminist writers and other troublemakers in the 1970s as the center of female arousal. The "clitoris" was alleged to be essential for orgasm, a function now known to be dependent instead on the acromphalus.

COLON, n. The light at the end of the tunnel; an organ of splendid promise and disappointing performance.

CORTEX, n. That portion of the human brain charged with game shows, cat food commercials, feminine deodorants, TV preachers, and self-service psychotherapy; although lacking arms, it is considered dangerous and wanted in California.

CRAMP, n. 1. Painful spasm. 2. Japanese surgical device.

CYANOSIS, n. Bluish hue to skin, usually reflecting poor oxygenation of the blood. A very grim prognostic sign, its name is derived from the Japanese word for "good-bye."

DEATH, n. The final effort of the patient to embarrass his physician publicly.

DIAGNOSIS, n. Eponym attached to complaints by a physician to convey the impression that he can actually do something about them.

DIE, v. Physicians never say this word, partly because they have so many synonyms to choose from—e.g. expire, pass away, be taken, go to one's reward, turn up one's toes, go West, cross the Stygian ferry, shuffle off to Buffalo, hop the twig, buy the farm, bite the dust, kick the bucket, beat the chicken, go to Davy Jones's locker, feed the flowers, cool, croak, box, beam up.

DIGLOSSIA, n. The anomaly of having two tongues. If both tongues are forked, you have a complete table setting in your mouth.

DISINFECT, v. To kill germs by physical or chemical means. Common disinfectants include chlorine, iodine, alcohol, sulphuric acid, napalm, formaldehyde, and Listerine. We personally favor tequila, which not only sterilizes everything it touches or is breathed upon, but also bestows a warm glow of accomplishment, a lift to the feet, and a steadiness to the hands, especially before surgery.

DOCTOR, n. Member of a small group of almost perfect people charged with high duties and occasional misdemeanors; v. To adjust facts to account for a greater reality or need, as in income tax returns.

DOCTORS' LOUNGE, n. So what? They've earned it. *You* go through medical school, internship, and residency, and see if you don't want to lie around once in a while.

ECHOLALIA, n. The involuntary, parrot-like repetition of words and phrases spoken by others, frequently associated with twitching and unusual eye movements; seen in catatonic schizophrenia and State Department press briefings.

ECMESIA, n. The intermittent inability to remember recent events, although the memory of events before and after may not be impaired. This syndrome is classically seen in early senility, but may also have an infectious origin, as suggested by the ecmesia epidemic during the Watergate hearings.

ECSTROPHY, n. The medical term for turning an organ inside out. While ecstrophy may be safely and easily accomplished in one's own back yard with organs such as the stomach, esophagus, or bladder, it is advisable to forgo attempting ecstrophy with organs such as the prostate or the kidneys, unless accompanied by an expert skilled in handling such tissues.

EGOMANIAC, n. Psychologically disturbed patient who will not stop talking about his problems. We refer all such patients directly to psychiatrists.

ELBOW, n. The joint between the upper arm and the forearm. Look closely at that loose, spongy, wrinkled bag of skin around the elbow when the arm is straight. It is the ugliest part of your body. It makes us sick even to think about it.

EMETIC, n. Agent to induce vomiting. See **ELBOW.**

ERUCTATION, n. The act of belching; signal from a high school athlete that a meal is over or a romance has begun.

ETHER, n. The first anesthesia, replaced in the mid-twentieth century by television game shows.

EXAMINATION ROOM, n. Theater.

EXAMINATION ROOM, PSYCHIATRIC, n. Theater of the absurd.

EXAMINATION ROOM, RADIOLOGICAL, n. X-rated theater.

EXAMINATION ROOM, SURGICAL, n. Drive-in theater.

FEVER, n. Infection's way of announcing, "Honey, I'm hoooome."

FRIGIDITY, n. The absence of sexual desire. In classical Freudian terms, frigidity is understood to be a displacement of the much more fundamental fear of egg salad on a bulky roll. More recent theorists have suggested that sexual frigidity may result from family curses, too many Bergman movies, or just the bad luck of being in the wrong place at the wrong time.

GESTATION, n. Pregnancy arising from a practical joke, such as putting a pinhole in a diaphragm.

HEALTH, n. Condition in which the physician is so incompetent he cannot identify the disease(s) at work. This diagnosis is a strong indication for changing doctors.

HIPPOCAMPUS, n. Fat farm.

HIPPOCRATES, n. The father of medicine. The mother is not known, but she is believed to have been a golf pro.

HYPERVENTILATE, v. To breathe deeply and rapidly without pause, as an expression of anxiety. This tactic lowers the level of carbon dioxide in the blood, producing dizziness, numbness of the hand, tingling around the mouth, trembling of the limbs, and a rapid, faint heartbeat. If you work at it, you can pass out. For a complete set of these and other exercises you can do in the lavatory at work, send five dollars for our free booklet, "Twenty Days to Feeling Funny."

IATROGENIC, adj. Referring to any disorder or disease arising as a complication of medical care. Virtually unknown in this century if you ask the American Medical Association.

IDIOPATHIC, adj. Referring to entities with origins that are unknown or cannot be explained, such as diseases like lethal midline granuloma or punk rock songs like "I'm Turning Japanese."

IMPOTENCE, n. Inability of the male to have intercourse the normal physiological maximum of once per night. Maybe twice. May mean cancer, and the appropriate response is understanding, kindness, and something to eat.

KINESIA, n. See **AKINESIA.**

KNEECAP, n. 1. Form of persuasion unique to modern Italian politics. 2. A drink poured across the legs shortly before retiring to bed.

LABYRINTH, n. 1. Intricate communicating pathways of the inner ear. 2. The floor plan of any major American hospital. Lost visitors are often used for organ transplants.

LANDOUZY-DEJERINE DISEASE, n. Complete atrophy of the muscles of one side of the face. This material will be on the final exam.

LAPAROTOMY, n. Surgical procedure in which the abdomen is explored for an unknown source of disease; technique by which the physician calls the hypochondriac's bluff.

LIPOPEXIA, n. A medical term referring to the storage of fat. We suggest a basement closet protected from sunlight and moths.

MALPRACTICE, n. According to your current doctor, medicine as practiced by all of your physicians before him.

MAMMOPLASTY, n. Cosmetic surgery of the breast; the triumph of hope over experience.

NAUSEA, n. Sensation experienced while the body decides whether to throw up or just die.

NEISSERIA, n. The genus of bacteria responsible for gonorrhea, known among doctors as the gift that never stops giving.

ONSET, n. Beginning—usually, of the end.

OPHTHALMOLOGIST, n. Specialist who looks in your eyes while robbing you blind.

ORTHODONTIST, n. Dentist who puts metal in your mouth while removing coin from your pocket.

PALM, n. Inner surface of the hand, subject to many disorders, notably *palmar pruritus*—literally, itchy palms, a common problem among physicians. This disease is responsive only to rapid and repeated injections of gold into tax shelters.

PENIS, n. The male sexual organ. Vestigial with respect to its original function of grasping branches while swinging in trees, it now serves principally as a conversation piece, except in California's Marin County, where conversation does not exist.

PHLEGM, n. Sputum or mucus; a medical term developed to trip up precocious children in spelling bees.

PHYSICAL THERAPY, n. A massagenous ritual by which nubile young women remind critically ill patients that being bedridden isn't so bad after all.

PLACEBO, n. See **VITAMIN.**

PLACENTA, n. Afterbirth. Biological proof that sequels never live up to the original.

POLYP, n. Tumor on a stalk; the body's version of Long Beach Island, New Jersey.

POUCH OF DOUGLAS, n. A small pouch between the uterus and the rectum, of little use and less interest. However, considerable curiosity persists in the scientific community about just what Dr. Douglas was doing poking around in there.

PROCREATE, v. To bring forth young. The opposite of recreate.

PROGNOSIS, n. Physician's best guess at how much time you have left.

PROSTATE, n. Never order this in a Chinese restaurant.

PROTEIN, n. Class of nitrogen-containing compounds once thought to be nutritionally important; now known to be useful primarily as a shampoo additive.

PTYALISM, n. Excessive salivation, seen in rabies and pregnancy; one reason you should always keep a body of water between a pregnant woman and yourself.

PUBERTY, n. A hair-raising experience.

PURULENT, adj. Full of pus. Term developed to save doctors from embarrassing themselves by making an indecent adjective out of the word "pus." A noble experiment in a lost cause.

QUACK, n. Physician who sticks obstinately by absurd theories that we do not entertain.

RABIES, n. Viral inflammation of the brain contracted by kissing dogs on the lips.

REFERRAL, n. An act whereby one physician attests to the high temperature of a case and passes it on to another.

REMISSION, n. Spontaneous abatement of a disease's symptoms occurring so unexpectedly that the doctors involved are unable to claim credit for it.

RHINERYNTER, n. An elastic bag used for dilating the nostrils. Honest.

RIGA'S DISEASE, n. A little ulcer under the tongue; can come from kissing doorknobs.

SCATOLOGY, n. The study of feces. No kidding.

SECOND OPINION, n. Another throw of the medical dice.

SEX, n. Behavior related to reproduction. Currently, that is. In prehistoric times, sex was employed principally as a form of greeting between nomadic tribes. In 10,000 B.C., the handshake was invented in the region now known as New Brunswick, Mesopotamia. Sexual intercourse as a form of greeting completely ceased, as the handshake conveyed friendliness without forcing one to get as sweaty, as in the old days. A world away, the Chinese were growing tired of reproduction by movable type, the compass, and gunpowder, all of which they had already invented. They applied the techniques of sexual intercourse to proliferation. Soon other nations were forced to take up sex out of self-defense. And that's how we got into the mess we're in today.

SIDE EFFECT, n. Pain in the flank that comes on with jogging.

SPHERESTHESIA, n. A morbid sensation or dread of contact with a ball. Prominent victims have included Anita Bryant, Bryant Gumbel, and the New Orleans Saints.

SYPHILIS, n. In Italy, the French Disease; in France, the Italian Disease; in San Francisco, the Plague. If syphilis didn't exist, the Moral Majority would have invented it.

TAENIOPHOBIA, n. A morbid fear of becoming infected with tapeworms—in our opinions, a fear that is perfectly justified.

TESTOSTERONE, n. An Italian vitamin.

TOMOMANIA, n. The abnormal desire to operate or to be operated upon. There is an immediate electricity when a tomomaniac surgeon and a similarly afflicted patient spot each other across a crowded room. Till death do them part.

TRACHEOTOMY, n. Means never having to say you're sorry.

TRICHINOSIS, n. A pig's revenge.

TRUSS, n. An elastic band designed to restrain abdominal contents and prevent devastation of the countryside.

UNDINISM, n. The awakening of sexual desire by running water. Those afflicted with this preoccupation are easily spotted by their ecstatic expressions at Niagara Falls. Often accompanied by an abnormal fear of Hoover Dam.

VAGINA, n. Aren't you a little old to be looking up words like this?

VEGETATIVE STATE, n. Blunting of emotions and slowing of other intellectual functions seen in most heterosexual men upon confronting salads made with avocadoes, cottage cheese, or beets.

VIRUS, n. Agents causing all diseases doctors can't explain or cure with a pill.

VITAMIN, n. See **PLACEBO.**